OBLIVION OF BEING: A Short Story

John C. Woodcock

Copyright © 2015

by

John C. Woodcock

All Rights Reserved

ISBN 978-1514285954

CONTENTS

CUT OFF

Every soul, in order to become a free, self-moved moral agent, must first go through this purely negative experience—must be 'becalmed', i.e. lose all its bearings, all its motives and springs of action, its very raison d'être and which now has indeed to decide for itself the stark question 'To be or not to be'. Every soul is faced at some time with this problem of transition from obedience ... to instinct, to the Law, or to a categorical imperative ... to free imitation.

In the darkened room, a single spotlight slowly strengthened its focus onto the blackened stage and the black curtain in the rear. In front of the curtain stood the master puppeteer, also dressed in black. His hands and face stood out in sharp contrast and the audience could clearly see the cross-sticks and strings hanging down, joined to the articulated limbs of the puppet who stood nearly as high as the master puppeteer. His eyes were wide open and guileless and he wore a cheerful, slightly silly grin. He bowed gracefully and slowly began his dance. And so the show went on. For an hour this wooden marionette amused and amazed the audience as the exemplary "ordinary man" that he was. He drank tea; he went to the shop and bought the paper; he drove a car and he met his girlfriend. Together they promenaded in the park. Finally it was evening and he was alone again in his kitchen drinking one last cup of tea before he finally went to bed. His arms rested along the kitchen table and his head drooped. He was tired and a familiar feeling began to creep into his heart. He wasn't sure that he wanted to go on. There was nothing about today that was different from any other day for Pierre. So why would he not want to go on? And what does such a question mean anyway? It was a vague feeling that came upon him at the most unexpected times and it was not related to anything in particular that he was doing. Most of the time Pierre liked what he was doing. His routine was meaningful and while he was doing it he had a definite purpose. So whatever the feeling was about it was not about changing jobs, getting a new home, or girlfriend. He liked Sally anyhow. And his home was a comfort to him.

Pierre just could not put his finger on it. As he thought this last metaphor he unwittingly glanced down at his arms and hands. "I have never noticed that before," he whispered. There, lying across his fingers and hands, were several strings resting casually on the table for a few centimeters before rising sharply off the table and up into the darkness of his ceiling. Pierre drew his hands to his chest in a nervous gesture of withdrawal. As he did so the strings followed obediently, without any resistance. But they did seem somewhat shorter. Pierre tried an experiment. He raised his right arm. The strings followed but now there was no slack. The strings were rising, as before into the darkness, only now they were quite vertically taut. Alarmed, Pierre snatched his hand back slamming it onto the table. The strings obeyed but this time, Pierre noticed a slight tension. He felt a doubt. He was no longer sure if he was moving his hand or if the strings were manipulating it. Manipulating him! He reached up to gently pull on the vertical strand but to his surprise the string quickly withdrew, maintaining the slight tension. Was his hand just pulled up?

Pierre reared up from the table, knocking the chair over, and reeled crazily around the kitchen for a moment as he tried to disentangle himself from the strings that he now saw attached to every limb. Amazingly, the strings danced out of reach, always maintaining a slight tension and, as before, reaching vertically up into the darkness. Now Pierre cast his gaze up into that darkness. He was shocked to see another face smiling kindly down at him like some great beneficent Moon. Pierre was mesmerized and his hand involuntarily rose up to point at this great moon face.

The smile broadened but was now tinged with a note of sadness. Two large hands danced with every movement that Pierre made. He could see this now. It was now no longer clear who was initiating his movements. "Whose life am I living?" There was no reply. Moon-face and the dancing hands gracefully reflected and directed Pierre's movements as his hands covered his mouth in horror.

Pierre's hands fell to his sides and his head slackened and drooped. The master puppeteer watched dispassionately as Pierre reached his decision. He looked over at the large pair of shears lying on the kitchen counter. They had always been there but Pierre hadn't noticed them before now. He picked them up and once again he and the master puppeteer exchanged glances. It seemed to the audience that a lingering look of bittersweet love passed between them as Pierre began his irreversible actions. Starting with his feet and working his way up, Pierre slowly and methodically cut each string that tied him to the puppeteer's hands. As he did so each limb lost its animation and collapsed, heap-like, until, finally, the little wooden puppet that had been known as Pierre, was hanging by just one hand, the hand holding the shears, and one string. As the shears severed that final string, they dropped from the now useless hand and fell to the stage floor along with the crumpled remains of the puppet.

The lights went out and the curtain fell.

"That was quite a show," Peter said. The three friends were settled around a table in the lounge of The Weary

Traveller, a small pub often frequented by late night theatregoers and revelers. "Here's to that sentiment," rejoined David and they all raised their glasses in a mock toast–two schooners of amber beer clinking with one small gin and tonic. Lisel always had a gin and tonic, at least in public, because only that drink matched the debonair gracefulness that she had been carefully cultivating for many years now. To avoid being considered straight laced, however, she allowed a small sliver of the world-weary slut to show through in the way that her hairstyle spilled seductively over her left eye–the degree of seduction of course being carefully managed by her hair salon consultant.

Peter and Lisel were the best of friends even though, at first glance, they could not be a better example of the "odd couple". Where Lisel attended assiduously to every last item of her person and garb, down to every careless throwaway detail, Peter lurched his way between his preferred destinations of almost any computer station. Once there, ensconced in the mode of being known as "computer user", Peter was at home. Here he could travel almost anywhere with complete freedom without the unnecessary encumbrance of his physical body, save that aspect known as the sensory nervous system. His body thus resigned itself to perpetual inactivity and it's inner necessity for movement became reduced to a radial one only. But here Peter's secret affinity for Lisel's world was revealed after all. Fashion came to the rescue. His unshaven face could be reframed as a stubbly beard, conveniently hiding his double chin, at least when seen front on, which was his preference anyway, a preference that he could easily manipulate to his advantage. He bought the best shirts and jackets that were designed to look crumpled, even disheveled, while his unisex jeans, with their built-in obsolescence, had the enormous advantage of looking old and worn, so that Peter could always wear them without wearing them out—CK already had seen to that outcome long before they left the factory floor.

Peter and Lisel had met David some time ago in the lobby of the very theatre that now presented the French master puppeteer. At that time Mel Gibson's Hamlet had been showing and the "odd couple" was very impressed with David's analysis of the plot, in terms of the evolution of consciousness, Heidegger's history of being, and the psychology of soul. The three thus became firm friends, even though it did not take long to blow David's cover. He was an armchair philosopher, a dilettante who took himself quite seriously. He had rather a large repertoire of disguises—ways to avoid exposing large gaps in his scholarship. His favorite device was to leap into mystification when challenged on philosophical details that he had no hope of addressing. He would simply appeal to an author that few had heard about, or indeed cared about. In this way David would appear authoritative and unapproachable at the same time. After a few minutes, any challenger would be stymied and forced to break off from the discourse. Both Peter and Lisel found this last trait endearing once they learned not to be intimated by David's inexhaustible supply of quotations with which he could pepper any conversation that threatened to get out of hand. They understood that David was not so much seeking any mutual understanding as he was in warding off any possible exposure of his many theoretical vulnerabilities. They each sensed a kindred spirit, a spirit rekindled with every mock toast that honored almost any idea or sentiment raised during their pub discussions or post-theatrical analyses.

After a long pull on his beer David relaxed back into his chair. "Well we could have a discussion about the art form itself. I mean, the puppeteer truly was a master." "Even if he did himself out of a job," chipped in Peter. "Don't forget the poor puppet," said Lisel, "your master puppeteer also made Pierre redundant!" "Oh! I see," retorted Peter, "this is a story of multinational corporations destroying the lives of simple ordinary folk. Is that it?" Lisel pouted and sat back while David went on, unperturbed by the wisecracks. "No, just in terms of the art form itself, what a simple but powerful picture was generated with relatively few gestures! Do you agree?" Lisel was well aware of the persuasive effects just a few subtle applications of shading, colour, or movement can have on the (hopefully male) observer as she spoke: "Yes I was quite taken by that picture too but what does it mean?" She leaned forward to show her growing interest in David's line of inquiry, knowing full well what aspect of her anatomy would simultaneously come into full view of Peter's line of sight. She was not disappointed. Peter was just at the point of taking another mouthful of beer when the eyeful that he got resulted in his stubbly beard catching the lot. Cursing, he pulled out a voluminous handkerchief and wiped his shirt and chin while David continued and Lisel smirked.

"Well it does seem clear that Pierre the puppet thought he was the agent of his own life. He went about his business making choices, being responsible for those choices, and accepting that his life was what he made of it himself. He was the author of his own life. Whatever happened to him, he created in the first place. Whatever came into view was a result only of his viewing it, his representing it to himself. That is, until he received a shock! Something appeared to him that he simply could not interpret as "mine", that is, mine to appropriate, mine to use or exploit, mine to know."

"Oh you mean he saw the string," cried Lisel. "Yes that was a powerful dramatic moment. Beautifully done!" Peter added, "yes the string presented itself spontaneously to Pierre." "Pierre did not *posit* it," interrupted David. "What do you mean by that?" asked Lisel. Feeling slightly ambushed by a perceived challenge to his train of thought, David scrambled to marshal his arguments. Philosophical authorities flipped through his mind like a deck of cards. He settled on Descartes and the momentous transformation of our understanding of Being that took place around that time, for which Descartes was the pre-eminent spokesman. The Heidegger card next turned up and he was about to launch into a long-winded exposition about the role of philosophy in shaping culture. Together, he thought, the team of Descartes and Heidegger should blow anyone out of the water along with their paltry challenges.

Lisel's question would, however, remain unanswered, while David was thus engaged in his private maritime war. For the simple fact was David most often spoke from intuition and only much later, with some quiet study, would *he* even know what he meant. It was this vulnerability in particular that had to be defended because, if David did not know, what would happen next? It was a frightening thought that he never followed though on. Thankfully, Peter, who was no mental slouch, rescued him: "To posit something is to make it so, as such. It is not so much a discovery or proof as a setting down. Do you remember in maths class, for example, where the teacher began an algebraic argument by beginning with, 'let there be an x!' She is positing a unknown (for now) quantity, rather than discovering one, or being surprised or shocked by an unknown x, suddenly appearing on its own volition, with its own intelligence, subjectivity, or even purpose. Descartes (Damn, David thought, he got there first) was the great pioneer of this modern understanding of Being. In other words, we human beings became the final arbiters of what is to be counted as real."

"The human being became the center of meaning," David almost shouted, as his intuition began to resonate with Peter's words. "So, if we do not imbue the things of the world with meaning, then they simply do not exist for us. The world and its things are no longer understood as bearing any intrinsic meaning that may impose itself on us as simple receivers of that meaning. The world no longer makes its own demands on us, or imposes its necessities on us." "On the contrary, interjected Peter, "the world and its things are now completely at our disposal." "Yes," said David. They were on a roll now; each man playing off the other's thought, rather like composing a jazz composition. Lisel loved their competitive banter and eased her way back into her chair, along with her replenished gin and tonic, in order to watch the unfolding game.

David went on. "For example when history emerged as a scientific discipline, the past was understood as a pile of rubble that had to be ordered by the historian. But this understanding was really a positing. The past was posited as meaningless in order for the historian to give it her own meaning. The meaning of history had to be imposed by the historian on the disorder of the past." "Yes," added Peter, who was somewhat of a mythology buff, "there was a time when the past, in the form of living ancestors, could approach and make its demands on the present." "Not so distant past, either," said David. Do you remember the biography of Black Elk from the early 20th century?" "I certainly do," said Peter, "why, that scene where the grandfathers appeared to Black Elk on the horizon, is etched into my mind. They invited him to speak, to ask them anything. He was shocked by the spontaneous appearance of these beings, and so, all he could think of asking was, 'are you real?'" "True to their word," laughed David, "they answered Black Elk's question. 'Yes', they said, and faded. But Black Elk's life was forever changed by that encounter. A true encounter between subjects! How different his experience of the living past is from our own modern experience of the past! How often do we complain that we never learn from history, that history repeats itself! We apparently do not see that our modern form of consciousness, which makes us the authors of all that happens to us, is predicated on positing the world, past or present, as meaningless."

This dialogue immensely satisfied the two friends. None of it was planned. Like jazz, something real came into the room as the two speakers played off each other. Lisel's cheeks were slightly flushed, whether from the intensity of the conversation or the concentration of gin in her body, it was not clear. In any case, she looked quite beautiful, and the mood in the room took a slight curve towards the erotic.

The three friends sat there silently eyes cast down until, with a short breath, Lisel blew away the stray curl over her left eye, which made her appear even more alluring in that moment. She broke the spell, "okay I think I see the string was not part of Pierre's real world. Apparently the shears weren't either. Or maybe Pierre saw something there but he had posited neither string nor shears as meaningful. So, in his world they simply did not exist, that is, at least until they appeared suddenly to him." The two men nodded approvingly, a little relieved that the silence had been broken. David mustered his vocal chords into action, "yes and for me Pierre's moment of discovery was the dramatic turning point." "I agree," said Peter. "Something alien intruded into his world, something he had not posited or authored. And yet he could not ignore it. It clearly had something to do with him but on the other hand it appeared as something alien, other!"

"He was shocked and then frightened," said Lisel. "I have felt that fear," she went on, "only occasionally, but I have felt it. I had a dream recently but it wasn't like a normal dream where I wake up and forget it after a few minutes in order to get on with my day. I don't know what to make of dreams. They seem to belong to a world that doesn't have much to do with my world or *the* world, the world we all live in. But this one was different. I don't know quite how to put it but it *penetrated*?" She cast a shy glance at the two men, being uncertain of their response and interpretation, given the last few moments that they had shared but David quickly said, "go on, Lisel. I think we're onto something." She complied. "Well, I couldn't shake the dream off. It stayed with me all day. It showed me as a living artwork, going about my business as I normally do, except I looked like an Andy Warhol painting or some creation of Madison Avenue. I felt afraid and it didn't wear off until the evening. It was me in the dream alright but why did I appear that way? I still think about that dream."

They all paused to take in this new information. Peter reflected, "so Lisel, after that dream you weren't quite able to go on as before, yes?" "That's right," said Lisel, "something has changed from that dream. Me! I have changed but I don't know in what way. I feel more … uncertain." "Well," said David, "that's how it was for Pierre, too. After the string appeared, and after his initial shock, he could not shake the feeling, it seemed to me, that the string had something to do with him, but what?" Peter added, "yes and Pierre did not just go on as before. In fact, he struck off in an entirely new direction, one determined by the string." "Yes," said David, "he followed the hint left by this new intrusion into his ordinary life." "He literally followed the string," said Lisel, "into the darkness," she added, now beginning to enjoy her own poetic turn of phrase. "Yes, that's right," said David, "and as he did so, his world began to destabilize, if you will remember his chaotic dance as he tried to reclaim his authorship or self-agency, in what looked like a battle of contesting wills, as much as it was a crazy dance. One suddenly become two and there was as much cooperation as conflict!"

By now the three friends had finished their drinks. It was just past midnight and they decided to buy another round and continue the conversation. None of them was sure that the various threads they had extracted from the plot of the puppet show so far would weave into a coherent pattern or, like some Black Sabbath concert, collapse into sheer chaos, but they were eager to try. The alcohol was the fuel for this mutual enterprise, and their discourse became its instrument of navigation.

Once again, Lisel's initiative re-kindled their discussion after the short pause. "Why did Pierre choose to cut the strings and why did the puppeteer 'agree' with that suicidal action? They both conspired to kill off the puppet. Why?" She giggled at her sudden surge of angry enthusiasm. The gin was beginning to make her head swim. "I think we should stay as phenomenological as possible here. We don't need to impute motivations to anyone." David was also slowly sinking into an alcoholic fog and, as usual, when under the weather, he began to sound irritatingly ponderous as if he believed that every human utterance was an occasion for profound philosophical interventions. "We can say, indeed must say in terms of the phenomenon itself, that the relationship was severed as self-consciousness emerged. And furthermore, this act of severance seems to have been intended, as symbolized by the shears that were implicitly there all along, although they were not seen by Pierre until now. Self-consciousnessh ishh, I mean is the very sheverance from a deeper connection with the other." David was beginning to slur but upon reflection he thought that what he had just said sounded pretty good. *I wonder if it's true though,* the unbidden and certainly most unwelcome thought shouted into David's self-satisfied assessment.

Peter broke in just as David was about to spiral into his familiar, but always terrifying, whirlpool of not-knowing. The only parts of Peter's sedentary body that still remembered how to gesture animatedly were his arms and they were now waving about, beer in one hand, the other raised like a policeman to arrest what seemed to be an impending stampede of horses escaping the gate of David's mouth. Lisel's giggles now threatened to explode into open guffaws and one hand went to her mouth, which gesture gave her the look of a seductive courtesan. Peter sent a warning glance in her direction. He was not to be deterred from his mission by any seductive and probably promiscuous wench. "Whoa, pardner! That's a big mouthful there"— this last being followed by another swig of beer, much to Lisel's merriment. "What are you saying here? We're all already self-conscious. That's what makes us human, you idiot! Are you saying we're all dead?" "Some sort of mass suicide pact," added Lisel now in open hebephrenic rebellion.

David felt a wave of paranoia wash through his being. Peter's bulk and staring, reddened eyes were bearing down on him like a crazed Minotaur, while Lisel the strumpet threatened withering humiliation through her shrieking mockery and scorn. His mouth was dry so he pulled hard on his beer, while his startled eyes never left those of his opponents, now possibly enemies. *Never let your guard down,* came the silent warning voice. Think of something, you fool. They won't wait forever. "Now, now." David feigned an armchair avuncular calmness." "Peter, of course we're all self-conscious today." He managed to insert a small note of derision, hoping at the same time not to further enrage the Minotaur. "And there is no talk of mass suicide, intended by evolution or some such, Lisel dear." David well knew how much she hated being called 'dear' so he wondered again why he might be inciting a riot with his speech. I don't think I am quite in control of this, he muttered to himself. But it was too late to withdraw so he went on, "no, I don't think the play, as a phenomenon, is an allegory of purely human events or experiences. Rather, as we have talked about before, I think the phenomenon that I am seeing revealed in the puppet show points to a transformation in the background of our existence or psychological lives."

"Transformation!" thundered Peter. "Yes, we've been here before. You insist that there was a time when we were not self-conscious. I'll grant you that when I fall asleep I also fall unconscious. I lose my self-consciousness. That's obvious. And I further concede that our friend Lisel is about to lose her self-consciousness right now." Lisel snapped back upright from burying her head between her knees. "I was listening," she protested, straightening her impossibly curly hair. "Yes David, just where is your evidence that we were not always self-conscious beings," she challenged, giving Peter a sly wink on the side. "That's right!" Peter blurted, further emboldened by this new alliance. "How can you possibly prove that weird assertion? And if it is an assumption, why do you need it? Liz and I don't need it. We're happy the way things are. I like being the author of my existence. I like being responsible for my life. I can bring my will to bear on the world and shape it the way I want. That's how we created this technological revolution, by the way. That's called freedom, buddy." "Be free!" echoed the muffled voice from between Lisel's legs, as her will finally sagged once more under the assault of a rapidly accumulating blood alcohol count.

David struggled to find some anchor, some island of sanity, where he could hold his own against this, what only could now be called a full beachhead aasault. He thought that a momentary appearance of truce might get him breathing space. "Yes, yes I agree with what you both say, Peter. We are awake today, or if you like, self-conscious. We do have freedom, and a free will, etc. Of course this is all true. It is, if you like, self-evident, therefore requiring no proof. In exercising our free will, we demonstrate it. All these qualities of modern consciousness are given to us. So of course we assume that it has always been so, that it has always been this way for us. In a sense, a very real sense, we don't have to be conscious of our modern subjectivity, we just have to be it and that is how it is for most of us in our ordinary lives." David was now warming to his task and gathering strength as he did so, "but I think that the puppet show is pointing to a 'moment' showing how this modern subjectivity that we all take so for granted, comes to pass. Not so much a moment in time, but rather a psychological or maybe ontological moment, but one that subsequently shaped our culture into its present form. "To put it another way," David said finally, "I think this puppet show is a picture of a soul movement, showing how our modern form of subjectivity emerges from a prior configuration of consciousness, one in which our human consciousness was still embedded in or interpenetrating with a form of being that encompassed it." Exhausted, David finished his beer in one gulp and leaned back.

Both men heard a deep groan from Lisel's chair. David thought that Lisel was evaluating his, admittedly highly contentious argument, and he began to rally the troops for one final skirmish. Peter, on the other hand, because his own self-consciousness was now drunkenly sliding down towards his groin, was sure that Lisel was teasing him so that it was his face that suddenly became engorged with blood. They were both wrong. "I think I'm gonna throw up!" Lisel quickly left the room and returned five minutes later, with a replenished gin and tonic in her hand, and looking a good deal fresher. Or maybe that was the fresh make up she had put on. The men dared not ask. Instead, they each complimented her, even to the point of flattery. In this way good will was restored amongst friends, even if it wasn't free.

"I was thinking while I was on the toilet," began Lisel, ignoring the startled looks, "about some of the things you said, David. We've talked about consciousness and history and whether one changes with the other but I think that for the first time, I began to make sense of some of the things you're saying." David melted. His paranoia melted. He wished that Lisel would also melt, all over him. I'm yours, he thought. He broke out of his reverie as he caught wind of what Lisel was saying.

"I agree that we all know that we are each independent subjects, and responsible agents of action.

And I agree with you, David, that this independent subjectivity is already given to us even though, as we know, each child must work her way towards it during the course of an individual life. Some don't succeed and we regard this failure as pathology. But we human beings do not produce independent subjects. Instead we each must achieve what is already pre-given us, how shall I say it, in our essence. In other words, independent subjectivity must already be psychologically implicit. And David, you're saying that this implicit psychological or background structure itself undergoes transformations that are historical. But because this background structure is, as they say, unconscious, we have no ready access to it and its transformations. Thus it is easy to assume, as most of us do, that our modern state of consciousness has been this way for all time, or emerged out of nothing, or at best it was self-originating in some unexplainable way, or worse, that it spontaneously emerged out of matter, as our modern theory of evolution would have it."

Peter exploded, "you thought of all of this while you were on the toilet!" He then felt enormous relief and the color of his face subsided somewhat. Meanwhile the puddle on the floor gathered itself together like the Terminator cyborg and assumed once more the form known as David. "Smart ass," she quipped. "Obviously I have been thinking about these issues for some time. I just use different language since my area is literature and the historical study of genre. We three have a nice alchemy going here—you with your immersion in all things technological and David's passion for the psyche and its historical transformations. In a way a very nice cross-fertilization is taking place when we three get together." Lisel was secretly delighted at how quickly she had gained the upper hand as she noted both men blushing and glancing away. Nothing wrong with exploiting one's feminine powers to the fullest extent, she remarked to herself.

Gracefully conceding defeat, Peter remembered that it was after all only Aphrodite who could succeed in subduing the aggressions of Ares, that plus the soporific effects of too many beers, probably. He began in a softer more conciliatory voice, "okay, let's go along with this line of reasoning, for a while anyway. I know you take all this seriously David and it appears that Lisel can agree with much of it through the lens of her own discipline. So let's stay with the phenomenon, as David insists. I am still in the dark about the decision that Pierre or Pierre and the master puppeteer came to—namely to sever the connection and apparently end the puppet's life. Does that moment also belong to the phenomenon of a transformation in the background structure of our modern consciousness?" Lisel quickly interjected, "well, we don't have to take Pierre's death literally, of course." Somewhat recovered, David added, "that's right! Nor do we have to think Pierre's cutting the string as a decision. That also would be a bit literal. It's more like this I think," and he closed his eyes to gather his thoughts against a strong desire to make love to Lisel, or if that was not possible, to simply fall asleep.

"I think it is inescapable that what we call history, in its raw state, comprises records—text, artifacts, paintings or other forms of art, buildings et cetera, scatological remains and so on, much of which has been produced by individual minds. But are those individual minds the same as ours? In other words when we read an individual text, are we understanding the words, their signification, their reference in the same way that the author did? Mostly we interpret the text and the world it opens us up to, in terms of our modern consciousness. So we're led to believe for example that the ancients lived in the same world, studied the same ideas about that same world as we do, but gradually got better at it until today when we believe that we have the most refined ideas about that same world."

David took a breath and continued, "this part may require some chewing over. We do have some historical methods that seek understanding of text and the world out of which the text grew or was produced by that individual mind. These methods involve participating with the original mind or consciousness that produced the text in the first place. It's not so much that we can become the person who wrote the text or produced the artifact as much as we can participate with the consciousness that correlates with the world that the text seeks to interpret at the time of writing. In this way our modern eyes can be opened to the way the world appeared to the author at the time of writing, even though the author herself may not have been so aware. Rather, the way the author took the world for granted in its appearance is buried if you like in the very meaning of the words she used. We can recover that meaning in such a way that the author's world may open up to us in experience. This reconstruction of a 'past' world in our imagination is what gives the researcher license to describe former states of consciousness, that is, the underlying or background structure that informs the thinking and perception and, correlatively, the way the world appears to the individuals living in that time."

Lisel's blood was racing now. Her mind was making the most amazing connections. New questions were flooding in, such as, what kind of genre of literature was possible with a given structure of consciousness? And if we extrapolated to modern times—this thought was particularly exciting—are there any emerging genres that could point to a further shift in consciousness and therefore world! She was not alone. Peter was making his own calculations: if all this is so, then how could we read our own technological civilization as a text? If we could do so, what would we read? What is the underlying structure of consciousness that correlates with technology? What is the "inner" of our technological world? Is that the right way to put it? They were now both caught up in the drama of David's account of historical consciousness. It seemed to open new vistas, new lines of inquiry such as, how did the form of our technological civilization come about, with its amazing advances and yet unimaginable costs. Is there a way through to something better, or at least something else?

David sensed that his companions were "on board" and he felt open to a flow of thoughts, almost inspirational, that started up in him. "If you accept the conclusions of the historical research I am talking about, then we can see a gradual, what shall I call it, emancipation? Yes that will do, from a kind of human consciousness that is embedded in a mind-soaked world that surrounded it, nourished and informed it, and at death, enfolded it back into its bosom. We did not actively think as much as receive thoughts and feelings that were perceived as autonomous, *other*. This is why the ancestors were so important. They were the wisdom of the blood speaking though us and determining us. A gradual emancipation from this "childhood" took place, punctuated by "moments" in which the mutual structure of consciousness-world were, as I said earlier, transformed—a discontinuity that led to radically different forms of culture. But the emancipation continued as human consciousness became more and more independent of, first, the wisdom of the blood, which got downgraded to mere "instinct", then emotions, or feelings, and finally, thought itself. This last "freedom" is expressed, for example in philosophy, as the "linguistic turn" and is marked by a relatively new capacity to reflect on language itself, which means, of coursed that human consciousness has, in some sense, gone "beyond" language or thought, otherwise how could we reflect on it.

"We are almost there," David continued. He was beginning to flag, as were his companions, even though they were both fully engaged now with David's speech. "What is the final stage? It is the form of consciousness that is 'cut off' from everything, even thought, no longer identified with any of it. And that is what I began to perceive within the puppet show tonight, i.e. the birth of that 'cut off' consciousness—full self-awareness of human consciousness's freedom from its source. It is no longer animated by the warmth of the blood, or by the feeling heart, or by living thinking, logos. We saw the final threads being cut tonight and the first emerging moment for that "cut-off" yet free consciousness—no longer animated from without, it can find no means of animation from within. No reason to go on, no extrinsic motivation, no external authority, no instinctual guidance! And so, as we now know from observing the signs of the 20th century, anxiety, uncertainty, and meaninglessness, and of course despair, impress their reality on the lives of millions, at least in the West. In reaction to these existential realities, millions begin the futile 'search for meaning', or the next thrill, or fill their lives with projects, plans or purposes, all of which simply betray the real status of our existence—nihilism, where any hierarchy of values has collapsed and one choice is as good as the other, since we all know that there really is no authority outside ourselves to tell us what to do."

The three companions sat silently. Their glasses stood empty and the ardor of this shared moment of community faded. Their blood, both warmed by alcohol and fascinating conversation cooled and Lisel shivered. "I've got to get home. It's 3 am!" "Me too. I've still got some reviews to do on the web, before I turn in." Peter struggled to heave his bulk out of the groaning spring-work chair. "I'll take you home," offered David softly, if somewhat hopefully. "Thanks buddy but I've got my own car," replied Peter gruffly, now on his way out the door. David was too embarrassed to correct Peter's mistaken self-reference and so he and Lisel kissed each other's cheek before parting company, she turning to the right towards the taxi rank and he, David, turning to the left and into the darkness of the night street. A violent storm was about to break loose over the city.

STORM

The death of the theologian's God offers us at least the possibility of a recovery of an immediate experience of the divine *that has only rarely been achieved* – that is, an experience of a living God with a presence in our world. Such a God would have an importance incommensurate with any object. As the source of our attunement, God would matter to us not just in the sense that our practices require his presence for their fulfillment. He would also matter as the being that calls us into the kind of engagement with the world that we would embody. He would, in short, be a God before whom we could pray, to whom we could sacrifice, in front of whom we could fall to our knees in awe.

"Dammit, I knew I should have brought my heavy coat," muttered David. He had a long way to go and the time between flashes of lightning and grumbling clouds was diminishing fast. "I'll take the shortcut." David turned off the street and headed west towards the mountains. He knew the area very well, having lived in the city for many years. West of the winding street joining his house to the pub and theatre became countryside and he could cross an open field, bend north again, and take a kilometer or two off his journey. Every few minutes lightning arced across the sky briefly, illuminating his way before the curtain of darkness enveloped him again. In the pitch darkness David swung his leg over the old three-strand wire fence and made his way to the center of the field. Large drops of rain smashed into his head and his shoes were getting soaked. Then, a bolt of lightning cracked across the sky, followed almost immediately by a gigantic roar. The storm was right overhead. As the lightning flashed, David was shocked to see that the field, usually so empty, held a small herd of horses. They had been watching him in the darkness and when the lightning lit up the sky they startled and began to pace in a circle at the center of which stood David, who was now too afraid to move. He nervously watched a kind of early movie of flickering shapes as lightning flashed, disappeared, and the horses raced to a new position, to be arrested in the next flash.

The ferocity of the storm and the startled horses seemed to combine to produce a vortex of sheer power around David, and he sunk to his knees, trembling uncontrollably. The horses' wild and panicked eyes mirrored his own condition and a thought crossed

David's mind that he might die here in this old country paddock. Rain lashed his face and white light pierced his closed eyelids so that he could no longer tell black from white. One bolt grounded in a nearby tree splitting it in two. The shrieking of torn timber sent the herd into a nightmarish gallop around the perimeter of the field while David's heart almost ripped out of his chest. When he could not bear a moment more, he thought he saw a ragged piece of lightning aiming straight at him. He had time to say, "this is it!" before the entire dynamic display of sheer elemental power ceased.

David was now in a kind of bubble. He could still see the storm raging around him and the horses pounding the earth and kicking the air, but within the bubble there was complete silence. Out of this profound silence—a silence David had never experienced before—came the lightning bolt, this was how David tried to think it through afterwards, but it was not quite the same as the storm's flashes of light. Rather, David could only say, "Let there be Light!" or "I am!" David was being uttered by that voice of the silence. It was not a voice belonging to the realm of the senses. David was speaking the voice as it spoke itself into the world through him. He felt for a moment that an *other*, to experience the world, perhaps for the first time, needed his sensory system to do it. He had the curious feeling of being doubled. He could quite plainly see the field, the storm, and the horses racing around the old paddock and, at the same time, another *presence* was coming awake within the sensory world for the very first time.

David was already on his knees before the majesty of the power display before him and now he bowed forward to touch his forehead to the wet earth. "O God!" he cried out in utter humility, awe, and joy. To his great shock, he heard himself uttering a single word that now spoke itself into existence through him: "David!" whereupon the bubble collapsed and David rolled onto his back, gazing up at the stars that were breaking through the clearing in the storm clouds. Dark rumbling and growling receded into the mountains to the West and the first rays of the dawn splashed into wet leaves and blades of grass, sending sprays of color everywhere. The horses had calmed down and now were quietly grazing nearby. David did not want to move. He had never felt so calm, so, … what was it, yes, at peace. He knew the questions would come soon enough, that his mind would resume its incessant activity of thinking, but not now, not just now, please.

Something had happened! "If this is what a true happening is like, then what is going on in the rest of my life? No, not yet, no analysis just yet! This peace is what I want, where I want to live." Yet in the very acknowledgement of "I want" David could feel something recede from him into the distance. The Light that interpenetrated with David's being, the Light that *was* David began to diminish. He raised his head and opened his eyes to see the Light recede into and become the morning sun rising over the hills and far away, momentarily blinding him. A deep grief overtook him and he wept, not knowing why he wept but he just gave into the sobs. He knew the horses would not judge him. This second storm also passed after a time, and once again David felt at peace, though it now had a different quality. He knew that for a moment he had become something greater than his usual self, and that *becoming* was, how could he put it, his *eternal birthright?* Then he lost it, or was severed from it, or it was withdrawn from him and he fell into his familiar separateness. And yet something has changed. Some residue of the experience remained. David felt separate, yes, once again he was *as* his familiar self, but there was something else as well, something that had not been there before the storm—or rather, David thought to himself, something *was* that had not *been* before.

LISEL'S DREAM

[Man's] submitting to his being without a God is his true humility. Man is here entirely for himself, but for himself not in the flat positivistic sense (of Dasein), inasmuch as now the whole former relation between man as upward-looking being and God as the goal of this upward-looking has been inwardized, integrated into the one relatum, man, and reoccurs as the inner dialectical logic of what being-human in the fullest sense of the word means ... the highest presence remains and with it our sincere submission, but this submission is no longer to a positive Other, to God and thus is no longer religious. It is a logically negative, a self-contradictory self-relation.

Lisel's thoughts lingered on the last hour of the conversation with her two friends and the generative questions it raised in her and in Peter, too. She felt warmth towards each man, though in different ways. She felt at ease with Peter in a way she had never known with a man. Although he too was no doubt a sexual being, he had downgraded the importance of his physicality in favor of virtual reality to the point that his efforts at seduction all too easily expired in self-deprecating humor. In Lisel's darker moments she also had suspected that Peter's adventures on the Internet strayed all too often into the kind of online "intimacies" that eventually paralyze one's ability to engage in real–time human relationship. She was scared to imagine the outcome of a community's privileging physical sensation over human feeling. Can we tell the difference anymore, she wondered, as the next taxi pulled into the curb?

David on the other hand, well, prospects with him were quite different, thought Lisel. She was quite aware how attractive she was to him and that she only had to give the go-ahead signal and they would both plunge headlong into a passionate love affair that could possibly lead to a productive life together. She was thinking of children of course but more than this too. She also felt that a generative union between their respective *intellectual* passions could yield a child. Psychology and literature had been divorced since the early 20th Century. For the past several years, David had been deeply engaged in trying to articulate how the texts of literature could reveal, to the properly trained mind, the background structure of consciousness that gave rise to the contours of the world that the text sought to interpret or describe. He called his method "psychological phenomenology" or "historical imagination", following the work of two of his teachers.

This work dovetailed into her literary studies. She was keenly interested in the problem of reference, particularly in post-modern literature that was replete with irony, parody, fictionalized historical figures, so that the reader could no longer be sure where the border between fiction and empirical reality lay. David was sure that this kind of literature was pointing to a transformation in the background structure of consciousness, an apocalypse of the interior, as he called it. He told Lisel that a certain kind of style within post-modern literature definitely showed the author participating in this transformation and becoming transformed in the process. Such authors often underwent a terrible suffering and their writing seemed to express the process of a new structure in consciousness coming to birth through the author. It was a structure, he said, that involves an interpenetration of fictional and empirical reality–two realities normally kept apart. Although Lisel grappled with these mind-bending ideas, she trusted David's intuition and was beginning to make connections of her own, within her own discipline. The genre of historiographic metafiction seemed most promising in this regard.

A loud crack broke into her reveries. "A storm is breaking, Miss," said the taxi driver, as he pulled over to the curb in front of her apartment. She thanked him, gave him a small tip, and quickly walked to the awning that protected the front entrance of the apartment complex. For a moment she allowed her longing for David's company to surface as another clap of thunder followed the sheet lightning overhead. "He'll be walking through this," she thought, "I hope he is alright!" She wouldn't allow her longing to go further, though, or she might have called him on the phone, to ask if he would come by tonight, or … "my goodness, it's almost morning," she glanced at her iPhone, realizing she had involuntarily pulled it out for another purpose. She shoved it back in her purse. "I've got to get some sleep for a few hours!"

Lisel took a quick shower, drank some water to avoid dehydration, "too many gins tonight, but who cares, it was fun," then she slipped into bed, naked as usual, but now with a wistful sigh at what might have been, "why didn't he offer to take me home, the idiot?" She lay there watching the storm unleash its fury on the city. She was well read and knew almost all of the metaphors for such powerful natural events, but this time she was rendered speechless. She had never seen such a violent storm. For a moment she heard pounding hooves and shrieks of battle before the sheer power of the storm rendered her mind strangely silent. Her last thought, before exhaustion relaxed her vigilance was, "David?"

Later, she dreamed:

I see David wandering the streets, alone. We are now in a hall where some ritual is going on and is conducted by an older man. Participants are each undergoing a ritual in a way that seems perfunctory, i.e. just going through the motions. It has a Masonic-Christian feel to it. We are all sitting on our knees on carpet. When he sees David, the old man suddenly becomes interested, more alive, and asks him to go through the ritual, which now comes alive. There is a line on the floor. He is to touch his head on that line, i.e. *submit*. He does and it seems that I do, too, as David and I have merged, as he/we intones the ritual of confessions. As I touch the floor with my head, the old man smiles and says warmly you are forgiven, everything. Then he comes over to me and crouches, whispering in my right ear for some time. As I listen I hear the voice of the *other*, a higher pitch, unearthly— an angel is speaking to me though him. I have trouble understanding most of it but the angel talks for some time. When finished I get up but have trouble speaking. My right hand begins to write automatically, I scribble "interlocutor".

Afterwards a younger man talks to me says this is the first time that ritual has gone for one hour, usually only minutes.

Lisel woke from the dream with a start. Everything was quiet. The storm had passed and the beating rain was lessening. She was sweating profusely and a mood of awe surrounded her. "I must remember this," she breathed as she grabbed a damp cloth in the bathroom to mop her face. She also had a strong need to pee several times. And she felt strangely sexual. Something is happening to my autonomic system. David told me this has happened to him, too. David! Where are you? She picked up the phone to call him.

PETER'S NIGHTMARE

Heidegger admits and fears the possibility that everyone might simply become healthy and happy, and forget completely that they are receivers of understandings of being. All Heidegger can say is that such a forgetting of our forgetting of being would be the darkest night of nihilism. In such an "unworld," Heidegger could no longer expect to be understood. Only now, and only as long as he can awaken our distress and our sense of our receptivity to a mysterious source of meaning that creates and sustains us, can he hope that we will be able to see the force of his interpretation.

Peter knew that his Suburu could handle the weather easily enough but the violence of the storm shook him. "I've got to Google it and find out what's going on," he whispered as the wipers slapped furiously in their losing battle against the driving rain. His headlights were on but all he could see were two cones of light illuminating the white strip by the side of the road. He slowed down so that his bleary eyes could see the road, a few meters ahead anyway. By the time he got home lightning was cracking overhead and the few steps to his doorway were enough to drench him. He fumbled for his key and cursed when it slipped away from his fingers into a crack between the tiles of his front porch. "Shit!" Peter had forgotten to leave the house light on so now he was in pitch black with no way to get in. "Where is that damn key? I've got to find it!" He clambered to his knees and scrabble about with his hands on the wet tiles. The rain continued to beat down on his back bending him further over as he tried to shelter his head under his massive body, so that he could at least see a little. Peter was beginning to tremble. The thunder seemed so close to him, right overhead! "Okay, the mystery key is hidden somewhere. Come on! You know the game. You're no novice. There's a button here somewhere. You don't need any fucking code breaker. You don't need to cheat here. Just find the fucking button. Shoot at the wall. Set it to wide spread." His fingers splayed out and began to stab blindly at the tiles. "Where *is* the fucking little monster? It's always in this room. I can't move on until I find it. I don't want to be stuck here. Come on! This is what they want you to feel, you idiot! You get stuck here and then they launch an attack from above. You know the game! Go into your 360-attack mode. I didn't earn enough points for that. My God they are overwhelming me. I need the key. I need to morph out of here!" "This is what you get for defying me! Bend over boy!" "No, Daddy, don't! I won't do it again I promise." "Damn right you won't. Not after I am finished with you." Whack! Whack! Whack! "Daddy!"

"Help me! Somebody help me!" Peter lifted his head up and howled into the night sky. His face was streaming with rain that merged with his tears of rage and fear. "I can't do this alone. I need help. Don't you see I need help?" He collapsed once again onto all fours like a sodden animal, and bowed his head. No amount of pleading could alter this course of events. He simply had to endure. There would be no rescue, no calming voice, no reassurance. Peter stopped crying and acquiesced to the merciless beating. He now looked down upon his body from a little way above and to the right. "That's better," he thought. He saw the terrible red welts accumulating across his back. He could simultaneously see his father's raging alcoholic red eyes from below as it were, and his clenched teeth. Peter noted the bad breath and the hissing emanating from his father's mouth as the old man's exertions took their toll on him. He further noted the young boy that was himself quietly and without resistance accept what he could not change. He was calm here. There was a kind of pleasing silence in this space. He could rest here. "What's the point of going back? It's whole lot better here. The old fucker can't touch me here. Yes, I think I will stay here. There is no one to help so I'll just stay here."

Finally, the storm passed. Gaps appeared between the clouds and a few stars glimmered through. Peter did not lift his head, though. He stayed there like a drenched bullock on the Savannah, with nowhere to go and nothing to do. His body was shivering violently but he didn't mind. Nothing mattered. There was nothing to protest, nothing to achieve, nothing to change really. It was neither okay nor not okay to be right where he was and nowhere else. And so he stayed as the contours of his front porch began to appear in the faint morning light. He opened his eyes and casually noted that his house key was right there poking up from between the tiles just below his nose. He remained on all fours gazing at the key somewhat disinterestedly. It didn't really matter that he had the key all the time. He had made his decision long ago. "Well, I might as well check the news and see how bad the storm was. Oh, why bother. I'll just get on Second Life and see how the others are doing. Silly buggers! I told them not to invest in beach property. They all know what Dylan is capable of." Peter worked the key into the lock and without a glance back, slammed the door shut after him. He ambled to his bedroom to get a change of clothes, heated his old cup of coffee in the microwave, and shuffled into the computer room where the rainbow-colored screensaver beckoned him cheerfully. A small sigh of welcome relief escaped his lips and he sat for a moment savoring the steaming coffee. "I hope David and Liz got home alright," he thought briefly, before mousing over to the favorites bar of the Safari browser.

INTERLOCUTOR

What is language, how can we find a way round it in order to make it appear in itself, in all its plenitude? In a sense, this question takes up from those other questions that, in the nineteenth century, were concerned with life or labor. But the status of this inquiry and of all the questions into which it breaks down is not perfectly clear. Is it a sign of the approaching birth, or, even less than that, of the very first glow, low in the sky, of a day scarcely even heralded as yet, but in which we can already divine that thought – the thought that has been speaking for thousands of years without knowing what speaking is or even that it is speaking – is about to re-apprehend itself in its entirety, and to illumine itself once more in the lightning flash of being? Is that not what Nietzsche was paving the way for when, in the interior space of his language, he killed man and God?

David made it back to his street in time to catch the odd looks of some early morning joggers. He looked like a drowned rat. Debris from the storm littered the street but luckily the power was still on and he could take a hot shower and get some tea. When his phone rang David was quite disinclined to answer it. There was nothing he particularly wanted to do. It seemed to him that doing, or achieving, or planning, were no longer important. Neither was he feeling hopeless or depressed. He sat there for a moment while the phone continued, until he realized, "that's it. I don't seem to have any criterion for action any more." The phone stopped and then started up again. Someone was trying to get through to him. David got up and answered it, still musing about his state of mind. "Hello." "David, are you alright?" It was Lisel and she sounded frightened. "I have been trying to call you for sometime. Where were you?"

David unexpectedly felt a flood of warmth permeate his heart at the sound of Lisel's voice. "Lisel, it's so good to hear from you." Lisel was quite taken aback by David's enthusiasm. Her fear dissipated and she felt quite shy. She knew that David had been long attracted to her but he was normally more reserved— they had exchanged knowing glances from time to time but nothing as explicit as this flow of warmth towards her. "Aah, can I see you?" Again the spontaneous enthusiasm, "yes, I would love that. As soon as possible! Something happened last night and I want to tell you." She replied, "why, that's why I am calling you. Something happened to me last night too. I had a dream I must tell you about it. It woke me up and my first thought was to tell you. I need help to understand it."

They agreed to meet at David's place in about an hour. They both sensed without saying that what they had to share required some protection or privacy. David thought for a moment of inviting Peter but a note of caution entered his heart and he decided not to. He settled down in his favorite chair to wait for Lisel. He returned to his train of thought just before he had answered the phone. No criterion for action! That was it. Yet, within about five minutes, he had acted. He agreed to meet Lisel. That was an action and also he had restrained his impulse to include Peter. Two actions but he could find no criteria on which to base these actions. Wait a minute! There was something. In both cases something happened in the region of his heart that led to action—immediate action and yet his mind could discover no reason, or maybe "cause" would be a better word.

David realized that he could not really consider himself as the author of either action, at least in the sense that he was so familiar with previously. He knew how to reflect for example on what he wanted and then to act in a way that would achieve his imagined desirable outcome. That's what we mean by responsible agency, he thought. Reflection then action for which we're responsible! But this form of action is different, radically different. I did not know that it existed before now. My heart *knew* something and that *something* was based on feeling, not a "should" or a "must" or even "I want". Action flowed from that knowledge, or maybe "intelligence" is a better word, in a kind of unity that I have not known before. It's like my mind is quite in the dark while ...

David's reveries were interrupted by a knock on the door. It was Lisel who spontaneously wrapped her arms around his neck when he greeted her. They gazed into each others eyes with mixed shyness and ardor that promised to blossom into passion. Again, David's heart held him back and he lowered his eyes in a spontaneous gesture that could only be called modesty. They both managed to step apart in the doorway and linger at the same time savoring the stolen moment. " Come in, yes, come in," said David, "I'll make some tea." "Yes please," said Lisel, and she made herself comfortable in David's favorite chair while he went to the kitchen.

David brought in some hot tea and biscuits, noting with pleasure how easily Lisel had appropriated his favorite chair. He sat next to her and they drank quietly until Lisel spoke. "I remember this dream so well. I feel I must understand it. I feel like I have been given a task that I don't know. It's a weird feeling so the first thing I thought of was to tell you. The dream clearly involves you and me in some sense but I know enough about post-modern literature to realize that dreams, that is to say the text of the dream *memory*, read as a narrative, holds references that are complicated, ambiguous, uncertain." "Quite so, yes I agree," said David, "but go on. Tell it to me anyway just as you remember it. Don't worry about ordering it into a beginning, middle, and end. Just as it comes." she did and David opened his mind to receive the dream without seeking to interpret it in any way, to let it, as far as possible, penetrate *him*, as it did Lisel.

When she was done he took a deep breath. "Well now that we've heard your dream, you should really hear what happened to me while you were dreaming it." David's experience during the storm was etched in his mind and he began to tell Lisel. He reached the culmination of his story—on his knees bending forward to touch his forehead on the earth, crying out to God, only to hear in the silence of his own depths, a voice utter *his* name, David. Lisel's eyes opened wide as she saw the resemblance to her dream. But she did not interrupt until David completed his story. Somehow, the depth of their sharing inculcated yet another virtue, along with modesty and humility—courtesy—the soul capacity to voluntarily restrain one's own impulses for the sake of the other.

Their mutual stories soaked into their being. Their gestures began to synchronize like musical instruments. A mood of playfulness entered the room. Their usual understanding of themselves as separate units, or subjectivities, disappeared and the *topic* became the subject. The conversation turned around a mysterious center that somehow gained more and more presence in the room. It was as if David and Lisel were co-creating another being that was coming to presence through their language. They both felt this, what could it be called, community? Yet neither participant wanted to draw attention to what was happening. They somehow knew that reflecting on this creative play would destroy it. Neither David nor Lisel wanted to be a spoilsport. At the same time, surrendering one's certainty as a separate subject carried a certain anxiety with it. There was a death experience involved in this surrender and both felt it. They knew they could give way to the fear and destroy the emerging presence in the room or, they could equally give way to the shared experience of their union, which carried, of course, a feeling of love.

There was no doubt now that love accompanied or maybe *was* this mysterious presence in the room. David and Lisel gazed into each other's eyes and the love intensified. Each move they made had to this point been highly improvisational. They each seemed to be guided from the heart in a way that was very unfamiliar in terms of what they had known about themselves and life in the modern world to date. It was as if they were being taught on the spot new capacities of relationship—capacities that were foreign to the modern separate self, yet were necessary if a new being were to be born through their union in language. The love in the room included a rich erotic aspect. David and Lisel's bodies were harmonizing; a rhythm in their discourse was clearly felt and intensified with every gesture and look. But again they each sensed or knew (where did this knowledge come from, thought David) that it would be a terrible mistake to ground this erotic energy in the physical domain, at least not yet while they were in the service of another being, a presencing that was taking place through their now undoubted union. Their union was real and their bodies *were* involved but in a way that scarcely could be described. The only way David could put it, and this much later, was that their very *speaking* gained a body, that a living presence was becoming embodied through their language which was becoming more alive, the more each participant surrendered to it and released the fear of death.

"What is an interlocutor?" asked Lisel. "My dream associates an *angel* with that word." Lisel's utterance of the word "angel" caused both to quickly gasp. David had long held what he thought was a very obsolescent reverence for angels. He knew very little angelology, and had long abandoned the idea of a guardian angel as just that—an idea whose time had passed. Yet, one of his favorite art pieces was Caravaggio's "St. Matthew" which shows Matthew transcribing the gospel as dictated to him by a most beautiful angel. David could not explain his attraction to this image but he kept it on his desk as the cover of a small writing tablet he had purchased at a museum. He had felt a strange joy when he read an art critic comment on the fact that angels portrayed in the mediaeval period wore the same clothes that ordinary folk wore. How strange that would be today, the critic added, if angels were shown in a modern business suit. The art critic was making a point that in the mediaeval times angels and by extension spiritual being was felt to be very close to human being and not all that different. Today in our modern times such an affinity between angelic and human being is simply out of the question. Modern depictions of angels and mortals are quite perplexing and troubling. David was particularly drawn to the art of Paul Klee whose angel series shows angelic being interpenetrating or fused with human being in a way that looks tortured or warped, as if some original intention had gone horribly wrong.

David had long imagined that the angelic realm required something of human beings and was pressing us hard but our collective terror prevents the realization of angelic intention. There was no one to talk to about these things since nihilism had done away with any hierarchy of values—what once had been called The Great Chain of Being. But our modern truths could not quell a deep longing that dwelled in David's heart. He never spoke of it but it was there.

Lisel had been equally drawn to the angelic realm in her own way. She managed to include her fascination for angels within the modern world, which had dispatched them along with the entire metaphysical world, by sentimentalizing them. She had collected angel miniatures, wherever she could find them, since childhood, and now had a very impressive collection. She had also studied Dante's "Paradiso" at considerable length and was thus able to entertain her guests with descriptions of the hierarchy of angels in Dante's cosmology. She studied Rudolph Steiner and could hold discussions about the various ages of man and how a particular angel presided over each age and determined what form of knowledge human beings could have. She could even speak of our current technological civilization in terms of the angelic realms, as described by Steiner. But, when challenged regarding her own beliefs, she relegated the whole matter to the status of "historical interest" or "childhood memories" thereby keeping her secret safe. Lisel, like David, was in love with something that she had not known to exist, that is, until now, in this room, with David.

They continued their play. "Well, most simply, interlocution is speech between two people," said David, "but there is an interesting theatrical variation of meaning, which you would know about, I'm sure, in which an interlocutor stands between two others and banters with each. In your dream the old man is whispering in my ear which reminds me very much of Gabriel whispering in the ear of Mary and impregnating her that way. As the old man whispers, the angel also begins to speak *through* the old man's words. Apparently, according to the dream, the voice of the angel is quite distinguishable from that of the old man, although it is hard to understand his/her speech. Reminds me very much of the State Oracle of Tibetan Buddhism! It was a demon, but one reoriented away from Power towards serving Wisdom and Compassion, by an ancient spiritual master. Hence the demon loved the Dalai Lama and, when evoked by the appropriate ritual, would whisper in the Dalai Lama's ear with a high-pitched, unearthly sound that only the Dalai Lama could understand. The demon spoke through a monk's vocal cords. The monk was merely the earthly vessel in which the demon could manifest in the sense-realm.

"All this implies that the angelic realm, at least for us moderns, is not so much separate from the human realm but maybe to be found within the human realm, at the ontological level of language, meaning that our task is to discover language as a way of being. So we now come to the question, 'what is language's *way of being*?!'"

David now lowered his voice involuntarily. "Maybe, just maybe your dream is telling us," Lisel melted at the inclusive quality of David's thought, "that the angelic realm is the very *within-ness*, or inwardness of the human realm—human *consciousness* would be better, I think, since our modern consciousness is linguistic and rising to the level of the 'cut-off', as I talked about at the pub last night." Lisel's body seemed to be vibrating like a harp. She felt David's words flow

through her and she immediately recalled a poem.
Without any consideration of the appropriateness of
her action, she spoke:

all aquiver
you reach for me, stretch me
anchor me to the four quarters
tune me
you accept my unconditional surrender
tightening, stretching
all knots released
pure vibrations flowing
steady stream of harmonics.

i can die now

breath returns
current courses easily
your instrument is now ready.
and so you play
and how you play!
music pours out
nectar, honey fills every pore

pause

you listen
vibrations sound off into infinity.
you are hearing something for the first time
and you need me to do it.
silence
you sit there in repose
awake in the utter and complete stillness:

awake!

my body the instrument of perception
of your creation
and so through me you experienced it

done, fingers loosen
casually drop me to the floor
clattering

i lie there
my body a trembling leaf

They sat there as the sun began to fade in the distance,
casting a warm yellow light throughout the room.
Cicadas begin to make their music in the bushes. David
and Lisel heard all these sounds, and more, yet both
could sense something else "sounding" through all
these earthly sounds. It could only be called—silence!
They waited … When speech seemed once again
required, Lisel pondered, "we must pay attention to the
whole of the dream, and its parts as expressions of that
whole. The interlocutor only becomes possible as the
other parts of the dream relate to it." Lisel's
considerable experience with dramatic form came to
the fore now. In any dramatic play worthy of the name,
every part of the play is an expression of the unity of
the play and is thus necessary to it. She went on, "so it
seems to me that the worn-out Masonic-Christian
ritual, and the dream-David's surrender and humility,
are also important to understand for us to grasp the
meaning of the dream."

"And don't forget the central mystery of *forgiveness*
that appears in the dream, and the wandering too"
added David. "Who is he/you/me bowing to?" said

Lisel, "and how does your submission enliven the old ritual, the old worn-out ritual?" They turned to each other as one, such was the depth of their communion now. They thought the same thought and now only had to say it. David gestured an invitation for Lisel to lead the way. " This dream parallels your experience last night, David, in an uncanny way!" David remained silent. "You submitted, you surrendered, you humbled yourself. Before whom?!" She was on fire now. "Through the violent power of that storm, you thought you felt the presence of Divinity, out there, as the inwardness, as you put it, of the storm. But you were, how shall I put it, corrected? Instead of hearing the voice of God emanating from the storm *out there*, as Job did, you "heard" a voice within you i.e. as *your own* inwardness, and what did it say? It said *your* name, David!" David could only breathe, "yes that is how it is!" And once again silence enfolded them.

David got up and prepared a small meal along with coffee. They did not want to break the spell of the moment that they were sharing together so they did not speak until they had finished. "I feel so different, Liz. It's difficult to say but I don't think the point is to *reflect* on my condition as much as to *be* what ever happened, if that makes sense. Some of things I have been saying today for example, and even last night surprise me, even though I am familiar with the content. I feel as though I know nothing, or very little, but that something else within me knows what to say *in the moment* and I speak it, but I must surrender to the speaking at the same time. In fact, this reminds me of a dream I had some years ago, a dream that prepared me for all this:

A. and I are in India, a dry dusty street of a village. I see Sai
Baba in the street talking loudly with great command in his
voice. At first I look side on towards him but it becomes
obvious he is directing his voice at me. He points to his feet
where the mat is. I am to come to him, now! I do so and
there is an old dusty prayer mat at his feet. Without much
ado I simply get on my knees before him and prostrate
myself. He continues to project his voice with great power, in
Hindi, over me. It sounds like an imperative of some sort. I
go to kiss his foot but he shuffles it away—no that is not
what is going on here, i.e. supplication to the master. Rather
it seems I am to be right there while he continues his (what?)
over me.

His voice is commanding and powerful. He is filled
with a presence and uttering it. Like John the Baptist! Then
he disappears and I am left there with villagers gathering
around and A. nearby.

Lisel agreed, adding, "Yes, there is a quality of depth in
your words now, and I feel we are actually being carried
somewhere by the words we speak. We are not just
communicating here but participating in a *doing*, in
some new sense of that word, I think." "Doing as
disclosing, perhaps," offered David. "That's a good
example, right there," said Lisel, "a complete surprise.
A new thought, and it moves me, takes me somewhere
I have not been before," "It surprised me, too," said
David.

"Last night we were talking about the puppet
show in the context of modernity being the age of
nihilism or the overcoming of metaphysics," began
David. "I am thinking that your dream showed that
"overcoming" in the image of the worn-out Masonic-
Christian ritual." "And in the revitalization of it,
although in a new form," said Lisel. David went on,

"Perhaps the clearest sign of our modern life as a time that is post-metaphysical is that we no longer submit to anything, not even the physical limitations of our bodies. We speak of freedom but never of necessity, which was a power before whom even the gods submitted. We just are not bound by necessity anymore." "It's interesting, though," said Lisel, "that nihilism is so marked by anxiety. The literature of the 20th Century is filled with our struggles with anxiety." "Particularly interesting when you consider that the word anxiety carries historical meanings of being bound, constricted—the very meaning of Necessity or Ananke," said David.

"Yet, both my dream and your storm experience show submission as, if you like, the *lysis* of the drama. In the metaphysical age submission was to the highest presence. But today there is no highest presence. All values have been relativized. We live in a secular age," said Lisel." "My storm experience gives us a clue here, I think, continued David. "As you pointed out, Liz, where I called out for God, I was answered with my ordinary name, David. "David" stands for "I"—the "I" of ordinary life." "But you were in total submission to this 'I'", said Liz. "Can this mean that the highest presence is now to be found in ordinary life or, as you put it David, the highest presence can now be found as the *inwardness* of ordinary life, no longer separate from or transcendent to ordinary life as was the case in the age of metaphysics. Maybe it is in submitting to ordinary life *as now* the highest presence that revivifies and revitalizes the Masonic-Christian ritual, resulting in the grace of total forgiveness."

David waited as Lisel's words reverberated in his soul. He felt an answer vibrating within him and he spoke, "and what is forgiveness except complete washing clean and closure to past sins. If we take original sin as a theological interpretation of our felt separation from our Source, primal guilt, if you like, then forgiveness, it seems to me right now, can be understood as reconciliation of that separateness and its source. In other words the Source is to be found *as* the inwardness of ordinary human life, as you and I experienced last night—you with the angelic interlocutor and I with the divine utterance emerging *as* my interiority or inwardness."

They were both tired now and as the sun sent its last rays above the mountain horizon the room blazed briefly in a golden glow before fading into gloom. They felt the presence in the room also fade and they were as two lovers falling apart into their respective separateness after a long time making love. Inevitable sadness arose, tinged with, what was it, yes, quiet joy. They had accomplished something and now it was finished. There was only the two of them gazing at each other in the darkening room. They each knew what would follow in the evening. It was time. They had touched each other so deeply and now it is time to celebrate their union. "We must discuss the meaning of "inwardness" or "interiority" or "inner" whispered Lisel as they made their way to the bedroom. "I'll show you another sense of entering the "inner", right now," David smiled. Lisel's quickening pulse and slight flush demonstrated her immediate willingness to be so shown.

SACRIFICE

Our only goal is optimal ordering, for its own sake: "Everywhere everything is ordered to stand by, to be immediately at hand, indeed to stand there just so that it may be on call for a further ordering. Whatever is ordered about in this way has its own standing. We call it "standing-reserve". No more do we have subjects turning nature into an object of exploitation: The subject–object relation thus reaches, for the first time, its pure 'relational,' i.e., ordering, character in which both the subject and the object are sucked up as standing-reserves" ... A modern airliner, understood in its technological essence, is not a tool we use; it is not an object at all, but rather a flexible and efficient cog in the transportation system. Likewise, we are not subjects who use the transportation system, but rather we are used by it to fill the planes. In this technological perspective, ultimate goals like serving God, society, our fellows, or even ourselves no longer make sense to us. Human beings, on this view, become a resource to be used – but more important, to be enhanced – like any other.

The first event that occurred as Peter logged onto the Net was a pop-up: "You are our 999,999th visitor today. You have been selected to be eligible for our latest iPad. You only have to answer these few questions and you could win!" Peter was an old hand at these scams. He knew that if he closed his browser and went to this webpage again the same pop-up would appear. But he got a small thrill anyway at being selected and pressed the little icon. He always did. He was whooshed away to another site replete with ads and "specials". He had intended to get on with his book review section on Amazon. He needed to complete an important critique that he wanted to post. "Well, I'll get back to that in a minute," he thought. "This survey could be important." It concerned his opinion about the latest iPad. Well, it's so happened that Peter had quite a few things to say about this device. With the latest innovations to the iPhone, Peter was beginning to doubt that the iPad had any real advantage for the user. But when he looked at the survey none of the questions compared the two devices. Instead he was asked about the choice of color, it's slimness, and it's latest security options. "It's your choice," purred the feminine voice. "Ok, I'll do it anyway; it will only take a minute." Peter could type at 60 wpm so the survey, even with its personal comments section, was a piece of cake. He thought for a minute about a pithy comment that could in 50 words or less capture his well-thought-out analysis of the possible obsolescence of the iPad. As he was about to enter it, he was timed out. "Thank you for your participation," she said, "you are now entered into our competition for our latest iPad. If you win, you will be notified by email. Goodbye, and don't forget to take a look at the many accessories for the iPad, right here, while you browse our store."

Peter was well settled into his chair now. Over the years it had conformed its shape perfectly to the contours of his ample body. It offered supple resistance, supporting his every move as his hands scuttled around the desk like two nimble crabs. He had everything ready at his disposal: coffee percolating quietly in the corner; a good supply of Arnott's mixed biscuits in case he got hungry; phone, fax, and printer, easily within reach; apps opened for quick access when needed. The enhanced retina displays of his two monitors had considerably reduced his need for eye drops but he kept a small medicine cabinet overhead just in case he needed something—he was prone to headaches after a few hours surfing. He kept batteries in the side drawer so that he could quickly deal with power issues. That was very important. Peter had several sources of power as well as surge protectors. He also backed up everything on the Cloud, just in case of disaster. He didn't want to lose his work again. It had happened before and Peter was bereft. He had, he admitted to himself, panicked. Years of work, reviews in progress, bookmarks, passwords, the book he swore to finish one day, contacts, email addresses—all gone! He didn't know what to do. No, it was more serious than that. He no longer knew how to *be*. Everything that meant something to him was gone—including the ground under his feet. An abyss opened up briefly and he was horrified. The only way he could think what was happening to him was to say that the world he inhabited had disappeared, and, in its disappearance, it had momentarily become evident *as* a world in the first place—a world that he now briefly and terrifyingly had glimpsed as *groundless*!

All he could think of doing was to restore his online connection as fast as possible. He could not bother with his old computer, the one that had crashed. He simply went out and bought the latest machines along with their most advanced accessories. It took him weeks to restore his sanity. The most important thing was to recover his passwords and reset them. It also talk him weeks to customize his machine so that is responded to his individual commands and shortcuts. It was vital to personalize the layout as well. He wanted, no, needed the desktop to look just the way he had it before. He needed that familiarity. Finally it was done and Peter felt at home once more. Everything was in its place and had its order so that he could work most efficiently. He was once again connected!

Now, this morning after the storm, having finished the survey, Peter was about to click on the Amazon icon when he remembered, "I must Google the weather. I need to check that storm out, see what happened last night. It seemed pretty bad but I need to know for sure." He quickly found his way to the local weather map and looked at the comforting icons winking and telling him what had really happened last night. There had been a low-pressure system over the city and it sat there for hours. Yes, the sea breeze was about 60 km/hr and it had initiated the whole thing, colliding with that warm moist air from the north. Unusual for this time of year, too! He could see that today was sunny and warm from the little sun that cheerfully smiled at him. "Thank goodness for that. I don't need any more bad weather." Small blue vectors moved up from the south promising Peter that some mild days lay ahead with swells 1 to 2m high. From his virtual vantage point, Peter felt invulnerable. He *knew* the weather but it could not touch him here. There was going to be no repeat of last night's dreadful mistake. "Yes," he thought, "I really should have checked the weather channel before going to the theatre. Won't make that mistake again!" For a brief second, the memory of David and Lisel crossed his mind but it was quickly obliterated by a pop-up that caught his eye. "Oops. Better check that message."

Peter began multitasking. His mail client was already open so he quickly read what turned out to be a notification from his Facebook page. At the same time he clicked the Amazon icon, taking him straight to his profile at the virtual bookstore, where he could access his accumulated book reviews. Amazon always asked him to review whatever book he bought and so he did. In this way Peter had earned some recognition for his reviews—or to be exact he gained approval from Amazon for the *number* of reviews he had posted. He was rather proud of that accomplishment. He had spent a good deal of his computer time carefully commenting on every book that he had purchased, especially his likes and dislikes. He quickly opened his latest review and was about to resume making his point when his Facebook page opened as well on his second monitor. "I'll just take a quick look at this," he thought. A friend had invited him to comment on a YouTube video that had just gone viral. "Which friend, I wonder?" Peter proudly had over 200 friends on Facebook. Admittedly he was not sure how many of them had become his friends but they undoubtedly were friends of friends of his, at least. "Cherie LaMotte. Hmm! Where does she live, I wonder?" Click! "Ok, Paris. That's interesting. Well, for starters I will accept her invitation to "like" this video and then I'll shoot over to it and take a look! I want to come back to take a look at her Facebook page, too." Cherie had posted a pic of a beautiful young woman smiling coquettishly at the viewer, in this case Peter, whose heart warmed immediately to this "close encounter". It held promise!

His eyes darted back to the first monitor where his unfinished review of the latest book was opened. "No way!" He began typing smoothly. " This author is clearly writing outside his actual experience. He has not been to war himself—by his own admission in the Preface, which the reader could easily miss by the way. And yet he presumes to be an expert on matters of military conflict. Sure, he has some academic credentials but what does he really know? The reader can immediately see huge gaps in his experience. For example, when he describes the actual conditions of combat, the reader is not persuaded. There is too much emphasis of statistics and strategy. What is the actual human experience, for God's sake? This author will not tell us. We only hear about the "war machine". Perhaps the author believes that the men and women who daily put their lives at risk for us here back home are just … " Peter's eyes stabbed back at his second monitor. The YouTube video was about to begin.

"O my God! 44 million hits so far, in one week. What is this about?" Peter saw a town square in a village in Belgium. Today there was a new addition to it that passersby noticed. It was a fire hydrant with a big button on top of it and a sign that said, "Press me is you want drama!" Finally a bicycle rider stopped and decided to take a chance. He hit the button and it happened! A drama exploded in the little town square: troopers roped in from the sides of buildings, a hit-and-run accident occurred; fights broke out; locals ran here and there, not knowing what was happening and at the end of three minutes of chaos, a large sign unfurled from one of the tallest buildings. It said, "and for the best up-to-the-minute news coverage, Channel 2UX!" Peter was electrified. He realized he was holding his breath. "That was really good," he thought, exhaling slowly. "I must send that along to a few more friends. They will love it."

Peter was now perfectly synchronized with his machine. The interface between user and computer was seamless. He no longer felt hunger or thirst and did not hear the signals from his body's need to urinate. In fact Peter was no longer located in a place that could notice or respond to any bodily happening. He was in cyberspace, moving near the speed of light, supported only by his sensory nervous system and fine motor system, which strained to keep up with his intentions. It could be argued that his intentions were in fact *not* his, not his at all. After all, in order for him to function as a user with maximum efficiency, *his* thoughts were not required, nor were his feelings, nor indeed his imagination. With the exception of the system already noted, his body was not required. The only capacities to be enhanced were those that enabled him to better follow the promptings of his machine or more exactly, the Internet.

It was the Internet that mattered, not Peter the human being. The Internet had its own way of being and it just needed Peter to be always ready at hand, ready to be used as needed. Peter as an individual was completely disposable just as his coffee Styrofoam cups were disposable. It did not matter which particular user was online. It only mattered that some users were always online. The Internet only needed Peter the user to be online. In a nutshell Peter the user's function was simply to turn the Internet on! In this way the Internet could *be*! Its way of being seemed to be nothing more than *movement*. It presented as a complete leveling of value. The various destinations users surfed to via the hyperlinks did not matter to the Internet. In this way it was completely democratic, or as some said, anarchic. Both of these terms, though, were quite obsolete as descriptions of the Internet's way of being. They were obsolete in the way that the word "war" was obsolete in describing the killing of women, men, and children by drones that were *partially* controlled by an operator half the world away. Drones were now also somewhat independent of the operator. Algorithms simulated a kind of independent decision-making, based on the field conditions that the drones' cameras recorded. No, all that mattered to the Internet was that users surfed 24/7. As long as users surfed, the Internet could exist, as its particular way of being, which was movement— sheer movement.

Peter could tell that the sun was setting at last by the nifty app he had downloaded recently. It was an animated gif coordinated with the calculated official sunset. When that time had come, the gif got into action and showed a bright yellow sun icon slowly fading and disappearing from sight. When Peter saw this happening, he reached for the remote and the lights in his study slowly rose to full brilliance so that he could continue uninterrupted by the need to find a light switch. He noted that he might have to go to the bathroom sometime soon, but not now. He was too busy. "Which window was I looking at," he worried briefly, but his cursor with its sparkling little stars that radiated out from it, comet-like, acted like a friendly beacon, drawing his attention to where he was needed next.

Without any further thought given to the distracting and troublesome grumbles from his body, Peter resumed his devoted service to his deity, selflessly and flawlessly giving of himself so that it may live. Peter the user was willingly being used for the sake of the *other*. His blood was needed by this uncanny being that was his lord and master and Peter gave it without resistance for he knew, somewhere he knew, that it could not live without his, Peter's, sacrifice. He was participating in a ritual like some modern Aztec prisoner whose bloody sacrifice of the heart was needed for the Life that was All to continue.

CHAOS

The experience that humans are structured by something that they are not themselves and that they cannot control themselves is precisely the experience that may show them the possibility of the insight that humans are needed by Being.

David and Lisel became what they call an item. Lisel
sold her apartment and furniture and moved in with
David. After their mutual encounter with the angel,
they realized that their lives would not be the same, that
another possibility for living had emerged, one that
required a new set of practices—ways of practical living
that they still had to work out in detail, i.e. if they chose
to commit to them. It seemed to them that committing
to their shared practices was dependent on a still deeper
commitment, i.e. to serving the angelic appearance, the
interlocutor. And in this choosing they were quite free.

They had both been born in the age of nihilism,
the age where no cultural practices are binding, and no
interpretation of human beings or the world are fixed.
Some called this world configuration, *chaos*. There is
only us and we have only ourselves. We are, so we
think, free to choose, with no choice having any
privileged position over any other, leaving us free and
at the same time, anxious. There is no longer any
guidance on *how* to choose. Many therefore choose or
make commitments putatively on the basis of personal
need, or desire, or on some act of reflection such as
"setting goals" etc. In fact we mostly commit ourselves
on the existential basis of our "unchosen" participation
in our culture's available shared practices. We cannot
possibly grasp the fullness of our participation in these
practices in an act of reflection. What we so often
interpret as an individual or free choice, is therefore
mostly the same kind of choice that everyone makes,
i.e. we choose from among those options that our
shared practices make available to us. Our culture is
getting shaped accordingly, with the explosion of the
advertising industry in conjunction with the economy,

in a way that deliberately arouses desire or need, only to have that desire or need extinguished in a product, keeping us all in a kind of stupor. David and Lisel knew that they, along with everyone else, were born into this world configuration. Perhaps *there* we had no choice, free or otherwise.

With this cultural background in mind, David pondered how he and Lisel came to freely choose service to the angel and therefore begin the task of developing those cultural or artistic practices that could give sensual shape and form to the being of the angel. These matters became a persistent melody in the rich repertoire of the two lovers' discourse. They both had a profound experience in which something *else*, that is, something beyond their experience of ordinary life had emerged and impressed its reality, it's undoubted reality, on their imagination. But was it to be trusted? They discussed the old Biblical admonition to "try the spirits", that is, not to be naïve in relation to the spiritual realms. Trust in their experience seemed to emerge from their hearts. They discussed the various virtues that had been kindled: love, courtesy, service, devotion, and so on and these virtues could certainly be trusted. They all had a venerable tradition.

Another way for David and Lisel "to try the spirits" consisted in evaluating the task they felt had been given them in terms of how the various practices they created in support of that task meshed or conflicted with the norms of conduct that already existed in the world that they shared with others. In other words, they did not simply abandon the wealth of tradition, nor slavishly conform to it, but instead they "tried the spirits" against it so that they could take responsibility for any departure in their own practice from that tradition.

With these early considerations they both felt they had enough to go on, at least provisionally, in developing those artistic/ethical practices that could assist the incarnation, if that word wasn't too encumbered by the past, of the angelic being into actuality.

The task seemed formidable! The being of the angel, that is, the interlocutor, is linguistic. Its way of being is therefore that of language itself, living language! Nihilism teaches that the linguistic being of humans has the background structure of the "cut-off" subject. Such language reveals the human subject gazing upon a mute and thus exploitable world—a world that no longer can make any claim on the human subject—a world whose being has been forgotten, or has been assigned to oblivion! On the contrary, the human subject makes *his* claim on the world, as he sees fit.

David understood something of the extraordinary philosophical advances made by existential phenomenology which opened our eyes to a uniquely human way of being that had been practiced for centuries, millennia, right under our noses, while our focus and cultural practices remained firmly on refinement of our *linguistic* being. Thus, while we now know that we comport our lives in intelligent and meaningful ways throughout each day, we also know that this way of being is *pre*-reflective. If you like, we just go about our ordinary business of life without reflecting on what we're doing at all. We just *do* our lives, intelligently and meaningfully, while, at the same time, we *reflect* on our lives and develop ways of knowing that have become increasingly abstract and removed from our daily practices. David had long thought that Being, with a capital "B" could therefore be considered as dissociated, at least as it presently appears to human consciousness—on the one hand *linguistic* being, as represented by the "cut-off" human subject, and its reflections, and on the other hand *world* being, including humans of course, which has become *mute*! Existential phenomenology has developed a language to *describe* this mute way of being, as reflected in subjectivity, but to date, Being remains mute and forgotten in the course of our daily lives, while our culture continues to follow the trajectory of this dissociated configuration, towards its inevitable culmination.

David's experience during the storm, along with Lisel's powerful dream, disclosed an entirely different structure, convincingly demonstrating that the being of ordinary "cut-off" humans and that of the mute *other* are in some way a unity. They both had tasted this unity of a dissociated structure when they experienced for the first time an emerging presence that named itself to them as the interlocutor, in Lisel's dream. Both David's and Lisel's separate subjectivities had been relativized to a greater unity, which emerged *as* the unity of their differences. But they asked themselves again and again what would be the linguistic structure of this Being, again with a "B"? How would this Being disclose *its* reality through the human subject who after all is its representative on earth so to speak? Or, as Lisel put it during an inspired moment, what kind of cultural practice or artistic form could express or disclose this complex and contradictory structure of Being?

Neither David nor Lisel could answer this question. At times it seemed overwhelming but both felt a task had been given them in this regard. The love they had for each other would sustain them. It was a steady fire that grew in controlled intensity as the weeks passed. They recognized early on that they had to focus on the nature of discourse in human relations. So, while they went about their daily lives engaging with others, going out together to parties, gatherings, social events, or listened to the dominant narratives in the mass media, they tried to articulate or describe the *nature* of the various discourses that were taking place in the culture. They sat for hours together trying to get to the essence of the ways that people talk with, or *at* one another. During the course of this research they of course became acutely aware of the various forms of discourse that they themselves engaged in with each other.

One of the first momentous discoveries they made, one that really shocked them to the core, was that modern discourse, if you can call it that today, was simply a linguistic vehicle for the untrammelled exercise of power. There seemed to be no end to its excesses. Public relations, the advertising industry, politics, and other major institutions functioning in the modern world all seemed rooted in this linguistic structure. They both felt that, underneath, hatred for the *other* existed. Or to put it another way, hatred of otherness dominated "discourse" today, as David once put it ironically. There seemed only to be desire to dominate all narratives with one's own so that any difference had to be eliminated. This was achieved linguistically by refusing to take up the others point of view. Rather, any alternative point of view was simply shouted down, or treated with dismissive contempt. A kind of competition between narratives was taking place in the media and in ordinary conversation between people. It was a competition to the death, no quarter given. The idea of surrendering one's own point of view, even for a moment, for the sake of taking up and trying to understand the other's stance, was out of the question.

David and Lisel were also shocked as they began to study the level of sophistication practiced in the media for the exercise of power within language. It was no longer discrete or hidden but openly taught as method. Almost every institution is being shown how to achieve its own ends through the sophisticated use of power words. One dreadful outcome of this prevailing practice is the increasing isolation of individual human beings and the sudden, often explosive violence that erupts inexplicably in the middle of the many banal activities of modern life. After long discussions David and Lisel came the conclusion that this violence, at least some forms of it, could be understood in terms of the profound isolation generated by a linguistic practice that utterly excluded any possibility of alternative points of view. Discourse had degenerated to the open and deliberate practice of eliminating any otherness whatsoever. This practice amounted to eliminating alternative individual appearances of Being, the consequences of which made the two lovers quake. After all, who or what is responsible for the effort of seeking to eliminate ways

of being and maybe even Being itself? Linguistic
genocide seemed to taking place.

When David and Lisel worked their way towards
an early formulation of *this* question, they both backed
off suddenly frightened, very frightened, and they only
cautiously and tentatively approached it again after
some further time. For now, after their preliminary
research into the essence of various forms of dialogue
between people and discovering the increasingly
dominant role power had to play in all the available
forms, David and Lisel began to prepare another form
of discourse that was based on their original experience
with the angelic presence.

They understood that the presencing of the
angelic being was facilitated only when their ordinary
subjective selves, which existed only in their
separateness, died or went under. This death of course
brought an end to reflection, at least the kind of
reflection that defined the separate self. Yet they were
clearly not literally dead or unconscious. On the
contrary they were each very awake. David discovered a
very useful analogy in the phenomenon of play. When
children play for example they are very awake and
engaged in the play. They know what they are doing
and can say so, but only in terms of the game itself. So
a child can say, "no, that's not how the game goes, you
can't move that piece there," and so on. But if a player
or an observer invites or forces a participant to reflect,
then that participant can no longer play, or more
extremely, the game simply stops. Such people are
known as spoilsports. For example, someone can
simply say, "you can't move that piece there, that's
against the rules" and the game can go on but if they

add, "you're cheating. Don't be a cheat!" then the game comes to a halt. Reflection is forced when the participant moves from the field of play to her internal subjective states of mind. Lisel added to David's analogy, "yes we see that all the time in the major sports. Play is halted every time motive is called into question such as, 'did he intentionally trip his opponent or was it an accident?' Play is never halted purely on the basis of breaking rules. Everybody knows what to do when a rule is broken. The penalty is applied and the game smoothly continues." "Yeah," laughed David, "what would happen if a player decided to contest the rule?" "Well, then," said Lisel, "there probably would be a paralysis of the game. In fact this happens in the legal field where a solicitor may contest the legality of a ruling made by a judge during a court hearing. The game has to stop until a decision is made about the ruling."

David went on, "So it seems that the form of dialogue that we are developing must exclude any speech that forces or draws attention to our being as separate selves. That's a tough call! Most speech today is based on and springs from the sovereignty of the separate self as author of the speech." "I know," replied Lisel. "I am starting to see it everywhere." "You could call it the speech of the humanist, because it rests on the philosophical foundation known as humanism. Descartes is the pioneer of this way of being." David went on, "throughout the media, we can see hardening of the separate self taking place. Dialogue has constricted to impugning, usually suspicious, motives to one's opponent. The subject matter of the opponent is almost never taken up and responded to. Instead we get a kind of erasure of the other by continually spoiling their bid to play." "It is this hardening that scares me," said Lisel quietly now, "it seems linked to the move towards destroying Being!" "I think it accounts also for the otherwise inexplicable outbursts of extreme violence that is taking place, throughout the West anyway. Being is attempting to break through the encrustation that is taking place in our cultural practices. Its attempts terrify us and so we harden those practices in an attempt to keep Being out. And so we avoid the necessary death!" David continued on from Lisel's thought, "I wonder if this awful process is what Paul Klee is getting at in his angel series of paintings— you know, Liz, the ones that show angels and humans mixed together in a way that seems warped or filled with suffering."

Lisel began to weep and David was moved to silence. Their discussion had taken them towards death and our modern culture's terror of the claim of death. After a time, Lisel got up, went to the bookshelf, and brought back a slim volume of poems. David instantly recognized it. He had written those poems during a period of ecstasy in which a crippling physical condition had brought him to the edge of madness. Out of that state he had written five poems. Lisel selected one at random and read it out quietly in the darkened study that was lit, by mutual consent, with candles only:

FOREST
you are only lost
when you know
where you are going

surrender your certainty

death will show the way

David leaned over and kissed Lisel's eyes, then sat back. "You know, the poem gives us some further clues about how to conduct the kind of discourse we have in mind here. I remember reading a quote from one of John Keats' letters. Let me see if I can find it." David's memory for quotes was prodigious and it served him well during his doctorate. He would not only remember quotes when needed but also could remember the source of the quote so that searching for the reference was easy for him. It saved him months of research. It only took him a few minutes to retrieve Keats' quote. "Here it is. It concerns a soul capacity that Keats called "negative capability" which he says forms a man of achievement: 'I mean Negative Capability, that is when a man is capable of being in uncertainties, Mysteries, doubts, without any reaching out after fact & reason.' Keep in mind Liz, that this was in 1815 and Keats was only 22." "Astonishing," said Lisel who had not come across Keats' letters. David flicked through a few more pages. "And look here. He compares the man of achievement with the man of power who he says has a 'proper self.'" "But what does that mean?" said Lisel. "Well, Keats says it would take five years to explicate his meaning, but I am pretty sure that to have or be a proper self would be to lack that kind of receptivity to the unknown that a man of achievement would have." "This is so relevant to what we're all about and you say he wrote it in 1815? Astonishing!" "Yes, and even more astonishing is the fact that Keats shows that negative capability leads one or can initiate one into something he calls the Penetralium of Mystery—a living center that appears to be another term for angelic being!" "My goodness," whispered Lisel.

A few minutes later Lisel said quietly, "you know, something is happening here, don't you?" David smiled, "yes but tell me what you're getting at." "Well look, you and I have taken on this task and been at it for weeks." "In one way or another," David smirked. Lisel poked her tongue out at him in amusement but went on. She did not want to be distracted from this line of thinking, not just now anyway. "I feel there is a kind of support or maybe even confirmation of our work taking place. Ever since we launched into it haven't you noticed that materials: books, clippings, news items—they can come from anywhere—as if a kind of spontaneous gathering around our work is taking place. It's like," she searched for the word, "yes, like we're magnets or our task is a magnet that attracts like-objects, things in the world that have something to do with the task. I mean, take the Keats quotes. You have had that book for years and now it practically falls off the shelf into our discussion." "I know what you mean," David said, "my studies have become highly focused now. Whereas before I would range broadly but without much direction, there seems to be, what, purpose, telos, which disallows irrelevant or distracting directions of research. I remember someone who had a similar experience in his historical studies. He came up with the image of a string dipped in a supersaturated solution. Crystals form along the string—another kind of attraction I suppose. He also described a certain kind

of intensity that went along with this kind of research."
"I certainly get that," said Lisel. "It's hard to shake the
feeling of being guided by hints, suggestions, with
nothing laid out as prescriptive."

David rushed on, "why, that reminds me of
another quote." He turned once again to his library,
found his old worn copy of Walter Benjamin's essays
and opened the Introduction by Hannah Arendt. "Yes,
here it is! I knew it! Listen to this Liz! Benjamin was
concerned with 'the correlation between a street scene,
a speculation on the stock exchange, a poem, a thought,
with the hidden line which holds them together and allows the
historian or philologist to recognize that they must all
be placed in the same period.' He's not talking about
some random process of selection but one which is
guided by that 'hidden thread' working in the
background." David slammed the book shut. Lisel said,
"it's the same process of a gathering taking place. The
outcome remains hidden like Benjamin's thread but
somehow seems to be guiding the whole process."

"Yes, that's right," agreed David, "the future
remains open, possibilities form, and I think the state
of negative capability is just the state to be in while they
form. Could be this is the way angels talk.

By the way Liz, did you know the root meaning of
logos? It's an image of *gathering*!"

PETER'S DEMISE

What are the Angels—the spiritual Beings nearest to men—
doing in the present cycle of evolution? ... the Angels form
pictures ... If we are able to scrutinize these pictures, it
becomes evident that they are woven in accordance with
quite definite impulses and principles ... Man must gradually
come to understand this in his wide-awake consciousness ...
But what would be the outcome if the Angels were obliged
to perform this work without man himself participating...
The outcome in the evolution of humanity would
unquestionably be threefold. Firstly ... the effect in the
evolution of humanity would be that certain instincts
connected with the sexual life would arise in a pernicious
form instead of wholesomely, in clear waking consciousness
... The second aspect is that everything connected with
medicine will make a great advance in the materialistic sense.
Men will acquire instinctive insights into the medicinal
properties of certain substances and certain treatments—and
thereby do terrible harm ... The third result will be this. Man
will get to know of definite forces which, simply by means of
quite easy manipulations—by bringing into accord certain
vibrations—will enable him to unleash tremendous
mechanical forces in the world.

While David and Lisel continued to develop their art form they had almost no time left to socialize. For weeks they were huddled over books, engaged in intense conversation, or moving about the house in silent meditation. They had the advantage of enjoying each others' company immensely. It was an energetic affinity. Even if one was deep in thought and the other was moving about the house tidying or cooking, it felt good. Their bodies were friendly and the physical presence of the other was never an intrusion. After a while they became so attuned that when feelings were present it ceased to matter whether they were located as "mine" or "yours". It only mattered that they were given their due attention by both lovers when they arose. David and Lisel noticed that they each, as a matter of course, often took up phraseology peculiar to the other. They began to understand the nuances of each other's humor and could often finish each other sentences. Most interestingly they began to read the meaning of each other's gestures and utterances even on a tiny scale, in *statu nascendi*, as it were.

With this degree of intimacy strengthening between them, the need to venture out into society with its many distractions lessened. Lisel still visited family and some dear personal friends but David was content with his solitude whenever she went out. Their connection was not dependent on physical presence, so that David found Lisel's image emerge in his mind at various times during the day. They discovered that on occasion a simultaneous appearance occurred in each other's minds. It seemed that their union was deepening on increasingly subtle levels. For the first time in his life David never felt lonely, at least for very long.

During this rather concentrated and absorbing time, David made several moves to call Peter who was after all perhaps their closest mutual friend. They hadn't seen him since the night of the storm and were wondering how he was. But Peter wasn't answering his phone. Neither did he call them. Melinda promised to go around to his house soon but time simply slipped away as the couple engaged with their task. And so the weeks passed.

Peter in fact had earned enough Long Service leave at the web design company that he was able to take the rest of the year off. He spent some of his pay converting his study to a self-contained unit, enhanced to be responsive to his every need at the flip of the switch or by pointing a laser. He had decided to work towards self-employment by carving out a marketing niche on Second Life. He was a software engineer and could use those skills to sell virtual commodities to other gamers. He had the brilliant idea of marketing home gardens to city dwellers. He would sell them made-to-order. This required, like all small businesses, a long 16-hour-or-more day. So Peter set up an automatic payment system so that all his bills in the real world were paid on time, ensuring that he had basic utilities working 24/7. He made sure that he had unlimited downloads from his broadband company and that his modems were the very fastest. He also had the nearest supermarket deliver his shopping once a week, again billed automatically on his Visa. He hired a cleaner to come in once a week and cook enough meals for him between visits, as well as clean the rest of his house. He lavished some money on a very expensive sound system with the best Bose speakers. All he had to do then was subscribe to several websites through PayPal and he could retrieve any music at any time. Peter had a preference for 70's and 80's rock.

As the days moved into weeks, Peter created many home gardens with plants from all over the world. Each was packaged with enticing options for the consumer. He even designed programmed insects that could be integrated with any package. He built a store on his own island and began a mass advertising campaign. There seemed no end to the possibilities. Peter's heart thumped as he sensed the prospect of making a lot of money—a lot! "This is real independence," he thought, "this is what it's all about!" Peter couldn't wait to get up from the small couch that he had installed in his study for his four-hour sleep each night. A quick bathroom break, get the coffee going, microwave the next chocolate croissant, and he was ready for another long day at the desk. At the press of a button, the heavy rock pumped up once more. Peter's senses were thus jarred into high alert and he intended to stay that way all day. His business demanded constant attention from him and the cocaine that he had bought from his buddy at work was a wonderful stimulant. He had hardly any need for sleep at all. That was the price for making money. Peter understood that. It wouldn't be long, he thought, before he could live his life exactly the way he wanted. Linden dollars were rolling in already.

In all this fevered activity, Peter failed to notice that all his resources; financial, physical, and mental were in the process of being entirely consumed. The rock music pounded his brain so that he paid no attention to the warning sign—a quickly diminishing bank account—as his housecleaner discovered his ATM card and helped herself to a raise. He was also getting conned on the Net by various others who had discovered the passwords to his many accounts. He had forgotten to activate the phishing filter on his browser. Peter's attention was solely on his computer screens and the many friendly little blinking lights that seemed to emit cheery little messages to him. The only warning that could register with Peter came from any change in those little messages. Once he got a terrible message from the green light one of his modems. It suddenly changed to a blinking yellow and Peter went into high alert. Oh yes, he knew this particular danger. The Internet was down! Shit! Luckily he had a backup modem through a subscription to another service provider. He moused quickly to the top menu bar, pressed the icon and reconnected his entire system to the new provider. The light on the second modem remained a steady green. Thank God! It wasn't the Net, it was an IP problem. It was a seamless transition and Peter relaxed. "I deserve a snort," and he quickly got out a straw to do another line that he had already prepared that morning. Now he was ready to work again. But first, more music!

Peter was drawn to one rock band in particular— Pink Floyd. They had one album, made in 1982, that he found himself playing more and more until it became his sole interest. It was the rock musical, "The Wall" and Peter couldn't get enough of it. Day after day he listened to it. He memorized the lyrics of the various songs and began to doodle a line here and there on his desk. There were a couple of lines that he concentrated on and soon his desk was covered with:

all in all
you're just another
brick in the wall!

These lines fascinated Peter. They held mysterious meaning. If he could only understand it then he would be free. It was a puzzle that he could not crack. "Bricks in the wall bricks in the wall. I know! I'll build a wall then I will understand." Peter broke off from his home gardening business and opened up some mathematical software. He quickly sketched a small rectangle. He knew how to iterate it. Soon rectangles covered the screen. But the order was not quite right. One layer has to be halfway along the previous and subsequent layers so he started again. "I just have to set up the basic geometrical form correctly and then iterate it again. He tried a "T" shape, inverted it, repeated it, and placed the pieces together, then hit the iteration button. It worked but Peter knew that that the array could be enhanced. He wasn't setting up the geometrical form efficiently enough so it was going off at the edges. "Almost got it!" He tried again and it looked better. "I can make this thing look whole lot better. I'll make the bricks 3-D for a start and put some movement into the whole brick wall. That will look fantastic! Shit! I could make the whole thing into a screensaver and sell it to boot. In fact I'll design it so that colors wash across the whole wall and the name of the user will appear on each brick in a pattern of the user's choice. I could even make a face appear. Yes a photo of the user could appear on the wall in 3-D!"

Peter set about writing the code for his new screensaver, using his own name and photo is a start. For a laugh, he went to Photo Booth and took a black and white distortion of his face in a mock scream. He inscribed the photo in the wall so that it would periodically and rhythmically protrude from the wall as if the bricks themselves were screaming, each brick of course now inscribed with his name, Peter. "Better still, I'll use my screen name, 'Grunt'!" All the while the music from the Pink Floyd rock musical pounded on his brain.

Peter's housecleaner finally placed an anonymous call to the police before she scarped with the balance of Peter's bank account. She was kind enough to leave the front door open so that they could get in. She knew that Peter would not be answering the door. He was too busy. When the police arrived and finally entered the study, Peter was simply staring at the screensaver that he had created. They quickly took note of the lines of cocaine sitting carelessly on Peter's desk and spilling to the floor. They saw what looked like a gorilla in a trench coat hunched over the desk. Peters beard was down his chest and his hair cascaded over his shoulders. The smell was appalling. They weren't sure if Peter was dangerous so they waited for backup, and an ambulance. It would take a few of them to move this behemoth, if it came to that. The policewoman eventually plucked up the courage to pull the plug on the computers. Peter did not move. His eyes were staring and he had a slight smile on his lips. Their attempts to rouse him were fruitless, so the ambulance driver gave him a sedative intravenously to be on the safe side. They hauled him onto a stretcher and drove in the nearest psychiatric hospital. They were pretty sure he would be staying there for some time.

"Well, we definitely have the presentation of a some form of catatonia. Is he violent at all? Do we need to further sedate him?" "I don't think so Doctor. He does get excitable at times and there is the feature of compulsive masturbation when he is in what could become a manic state. But there is no catalepsy so to speak. He's avoiding all eye contact and seems to be having some sort of internal self-talk." "But you don't feel there is any risk of harm to self or others? Maybe we could keep him a while on the basis of harm to reputation?" "Yes, Doctor that will do, yes. That covers us legally." "We'll give him a complete work-up, just to make sure there is no underlying neuropathology. I mean look at his weight. You can almost guarantee some physical component to this. Hit him with some Lorazepam. Has he had any substance abuse, history of depression?" "The police saw evidence of cocaine use, Doctor. We don't know about any depression yet." "Ok, we'll keep it short term. Just manage the anxiety for now and help him sleep. We'll see how he is when he wakes up. And maybe that excitability will calm down too. Then I want to think of possibly some SSRI's or maybe Lithium over the long haul. His self-talk worries me that there might be some schizophrenic features. Has he a medical record on that? He may need some combination to manage his symptoms if we are to get him back to some semblance of normalcy and he's got to have something to manage his high blood pressure. Let's think about Lisinopril for that. My god, the man's heart must be laboring. Be sure to get a history asap, please."

They were very pleased that Peter came back relatively quickly—the miracle of benzodiazepines! He still exhibited some waxy flexibility in his limbs but apart from high blood pressure, there seemed to be no underlying medical condition. After he woke up he was quite responsive, gave his medical history to the staff, and was in all things quite co-operative. His psychiatrist, a seasoned veteran of forty years was the only one to notice that Peter's compliance was just a little bit manipulative. He was learning quickly what he had to say in order to get discharged. Peter seemed to eager to be elsewhere, so there was some presentation of pressured speech, but he was lucid enough and related to his social context. The psychiatrist was further reassured by his knowledge of the efficacy of the medications that he was prescribing. They would smooth out Peter's moods, lower the anxiety, lift the depression and normalize his thinking hopefully, and help him sleep—four hours a day was simply not enough. Peter thus successfully negotiated the gentle interrogation of the Review Tribunal and was soon on his way home.

The house was quite cold and dark when Peter arrived. He did not yet know the extent of his financial ruin. He expected his housecleaner would come tomorrow and that his groceries would be delivered as usual so all his focus, his growing enthusiasm, centered on the computers in his study which was in the same state that he had left it two days before, except that the line or two of cocaine left on his desk had been carefully sealed in a plastic bag by the police before they left, as possible evidence. He booted up his computers, turned on the automatic coffee dispenser, cracked open a tin of Arnott's and settled in to his creaking leather chair, which seemed to give way in silent gratitude for his bulky presence once more. He spent a few more hours tweaking, compressing, and packaging his screensaver and then Peter the user a.k.a "Grunt" once more entered Second Life. Grunt quickly flew over to his store Home Gardens and listed the screensaver as a free option with any two purchases. He checked his account and yes, there were plenty of Linden dollars. It was time to get busy.

The first thing Grunt had to do was to clean himself up. He needed to bulk up, slim down and yes, add a few inches here and there. Now over to the 18+ section. It was time to go get a girlfriend.

DECISION

To say that the chaos is eternally recurring means that there is no fixed and binding way of relating things, no standing obligations to prior arrangements, and so on. We find ourselves constantly returned to a situation where we are free to rearrange and reestablish our own interpretation of the world. What things *are* is open to reconfiguration (thus, entities are unstable), but that they are open to reconfiguration is uniformly the case.

David and Lisel began to practice their dialogic art form. They liked to think of it now as a way, a way towards the Penetralium of Mystery. They were each shocked at first at the frequency with which their habitual narrative forms stopped the movement and they were snapped back into their separate reflective selves. Much of their early attempts were therefore focused on stripping away the kind of speech that edified the subjective self. For example they had to give up dogmatic claims of ownership—moods, emotions, and even thoughts, all so easily appropriated as the property for the Cartesian ego, were released with the result that David and Lisel began to experience themselves as being *within* the mood, or thought. David mused that the very notion of space was thus inverted. "And time too," Lisel said, " haven't you noticed how we have given up a causal sense of time in the sense that present events are caused by past ones." It was true! When they got into an argument for example, they no longer looked for the origin of the argument in an action in the past such as "the argument started when you forgot the keys last night." This form of narrative shut out any possible attunement to a "cause" that penetrated from "beyond" or the "not yet". They instead began to look for discontinuities in time in which the presence of an "intruder" or "guest" could be felt and to privilege that over causal accounts expressed in purely human terms.

They even found a picture of their art form—a spiral. This form could be compared to the dominant narrative form pictured as a straight line. Their new dialogic form circled around a center, which they call the Penetralium of Mystery, after Keats. But there was also a sense that as they circled they got nearer the center, hence the spiral. So, David and Lisel provisionally agreed to call the dialogue form "spirallic discourse—in search of the angel." But then they changed it to: "spirallic discourse—welcoming the angel." Probably, further changes would happen as they became more attuned to the process.

In addition to this new art form David and Lisel had another task: to *account* for the original experience on night of the storm. It had a profound effect on them and reconfigured their mode of being in the sense that "things" began to appear differently to them. First of all, and quite surprisingly, there were the *new* appearances. Things that they had not noticed before became prominent. For example, the operations of power that dominated modern narratives throughout the media and in ordinary conversations, to the exclusion of all else, had shocked them. Also, the hardening of the modern ego or subjective self as expressed in the language of exclusion, that is language that excluded any form of otherness, was alarming and later, depressing. David and Lisel came to understand the myriad of ways by which *difference* was fended off, dismissed, excluded, or even erased, leading to the stunning prevalence of crippling isolation. They both felt so grateful for the love that had sprung up between them and which now bound them so willingly together. Yet, at times, with these new and frightening appearances of the world, both David and Lisel nervously wondered if that love could withstand the daily onslaughts of power working its way through even the most banal human discourse during the course of an ordinary day. This power was no longer in the hands of the monarch, or any individual, for that matter. Neither did it reside in institutions like governments. It manifested, as Foucault says, within the ordinary practices of daily life and everyone is subject to it. He called this power, *biopower* to highlight its sphere of operations in physical bodies. We no longer need to be corrected into conformity by some authority figure. Our bodies, and speech, e.g. political correctness, simply mold to the norm automatically now.

After one particularly harrowing day, David came home and Lisel was startled to see how beaten down her lover looked. They made some dinner together and pulled out their best red. They ate quietly and Lisel could see David recovering somewhat as his body was nourished by the good food and wine, while his eyes drank in her lovely face and concerned expression. After a while she felt that the time was right to ask the question, "well, what happened?" "I got beaten up," he confirmed her perception. She waited. " I just haven't found the right language to say what needs to be said. When I give these lectures I am always left with the feeling that others already know what I have to say and that they are simply there to have what they know confirmed by yet someone else." "How did someone put it, in another context," Lisel chimed in, "the endless retailing of accumulated knowledge?" David felt his body relaxed even further. He immediately felt heard. There was a clear invitation to continue. "Yes, that's right! Whenever I said something familiar, or that sounded familiar, that is, I was using words familiar to the group, I felt that I was being shoved into categories of experience that I desperately wanted to avoid. My words quickly got assimilated to familiar knowledge and people responded from that knowledge, propounding it yet once more. The *unfamiliar* aspect to what I was saying got lost completely. And so we ended up having a discourse where people simply reiterated what they already knew. What they *didn't* know, what I had come to transmit in some small way, was ignored, or at times, met by a kind of silent hostility. After a time, I simply had to stop saying, 'no that's not it, that's not quite what I'm saying.'" Lisel drew the inference, "aah! No one was *moved* by what you're saying, or perhaps it's better to say, there was no movement in that little community of spirits." "No! There wasn't! Movement was blocked at every turn!" David exploded in anger. "I feel stifled, choked; I could not say what needed to be said. Dammit! There's no *movement*!"

Lisel absorbed this shockwave of violence from the lover. She knew it was not personally directed at her. It had to come out. She knew that it was not just David frustrated at not getting *his* point across, but in all likelihood David was expressing the suffering of the Interlocutor who cannot enter the human domain while knowledge is so usurped by power for its own purpose—what seems to be an all-out attack on movement, movement as the essence of Being itself—an attack that is frighteningly successful.

After a few minutes she said, "we have to deal with the fact, the obvious fact, that the people in the group, and I suppose the community at large, is not ill-intentioned, not malicious. The force operating through the network of human relations, which you and I call power, is not reducible to human intention. I think we agree on this, yes?" David accurately detected that Lisel's mind was lifting off the particulars of his grievance and moving towards more fundamental considerations. He silently acquiesced to this new depth of exploration. After all, this was an example of the spirallic nature of the dialogue they were developing together. He nodded and Lisel continued, "mostly people today go on about their daily business quite well, quite intelligently, without a thought for the Being of the world from which *their* being emerged and in which their being continues to be embedded, until they die, reflective consciousness notwithstanding." David added, "we live entirely on the surface of life today. The world appears as surface only but we do not see that view as a *perspective*. It has become absolute, corresponding to an absolute hardening of the subjective self." "Yes," said Lisel, "if we could understand that correspondence as such, the absoluteness of the world of surfaces would become relativized, a perspective only and therefore not the only perspective.

"Now, David, a question for us, one that I think relates to an adequate account of our mutual experience on the night of the storm, is this: how did you and I gain the knowledge that our modern world of appearances, that is, the world in which "things" appear as surface only, is only a perspective? How did that happen? How did we come to know that other worlds, other perspectives, are possible?" David opened his mouth to reply, but Lisel was asking the question rhetorically. She already knew the answer, "Wasn't it just because you and I were, in effect, initiated into another world. Let's call it the world of the Interlocutor, a world in which depth is no longer a void or a chasm of nothingness, as the existentialists would have it, but instead embodies intelligence, wisdom, subjectivity!"

"You could say that we overcame ourselves, I think," said David. "We overcame an entire way of being, let's call it, 'overcoming solidity', or overcoming the subjective self." "Yes that feels right to me too, at least as a start anyway," said Lisel, "but that is not all. It's not enough to be given a big experience. How many big experiences today are appropriated by the incorrigible need for a thrill? How much of what could be a transformative moment is usurped and consumed by the entertainment industry? No, something more is needed, and I can only think of it in terms of a *decision* that we each made, alone." David asked, "what are the characteristics of that decision?" They lapsed into silence, both pregnant with this generative question. "This decision is certainly tied to commitment," David began, "it has a central feature of: 'here I stand, here I make a stand, this is what counts for me, this is what matters, perhaps even this is what I am willing to die for. In this place I am adamant, unshakable'—and of course none of this stance is to be converted into an ideology that is imposed from the outside on others." "That's a really good start," Lisel effused. "Your description resonates with my own experience very closely. But there's more to this matter, more to the phenomenology of this commitment. As you will remember David both my dream and your experience in that field are centrally concerned with surrender, humility, forgiveness, all of which we have discussed over the subsequent weeks. Right now, I rather suspect that what has to be given up in order to reach the place, the Penetralium of Mystery, is a certain kind of knowing…" "Yes," David interrupted, "the kind of knowing that beat me up today, the kind of knowing that edifies the subjective self and isolates it at the same time." "We know how to *know* but we do not know how to *be!*" Lisel's newly created aphorism delighted them both. It was another instance of spontaneous speech that emerges at times form the center of their spirallic dialogue.

"What happens when that way of knowing is surrendered? Reflecting back on our experiences, perhaps mine in particular in that old paddock, I would have to say that the first presentation of the angel is a presentation of sheer terror. I don't think there's any way around that initial appearance for the modern hardened ego. "Beauty is nothing but the beginning of terror that we're still just able to bear," Lisel intoned their favorite Rilke quote. Again they fell silent savoring the precious words of the Master poet. "Much then depends on one's preparation for such a moment, I should think," said David. He invoked his knowledge of psychology, "I think there are many people who become exposed to this terror through some kind of psychic wounding, what you might call trauma today. Two things go wrong. Trauma theory today consists of causal explanations given solely in terms of past personal history. This gives the trauma victim meaning, from the outside as it were, and it is sufficient to weave an otherwise fragmented chaotic life into a workable coherent whole known as "victim". One can then adhere to this or other like categories and make it one's identity, one that is readily included and accepted by the dominant narratives and practices of our time. So, the victim is restored to society in its *present* configuration and, by the very same token, prevented from any consideration of alternative configurations. The second thing that's wrong in our approach to psychic wounding is that it is an *exclusive* approach, which is to say that any approach to psychic wounding that suggests another temporal factor might be involved, not the past but the *unknown future* is excluded from the start. The terror of psychic wounding is understood purely in terms of human factors 'located' in the past and this has the unfortunate consequence of raising the status of some human beings to that of monster. The monstrous or terrifying aspect of Being is consigned to oblivion."

Lisel decided to amplify David's thought. "When I went to India all those years ago, I was really struck by the iconography that I found there, particularly that of the Buddhists who had been exiled there after the Chinese invasion in 1949. The Buddhists do not hold back in their symbology. There are some simply superb images of terror and bliss, for example, contained in the one symbol. It's the same in the Hindu religion too. I remember one with Kali wildly dancing, with skulls rattling around her neck, on the living corpse of Shiva whose eyes are open and staring. It sure looks like terror that is being shown in the face of death and the dance of life. So much wisdom about the nature of Being for thousands of years, and now all forgotten."

Lisel continued, "individuals today are completely unprepared for an encounter with Being. And that's because of the oblivion of Being. In the face of this unpreparedness Being presents itself with the face of terror but still, as the Buddhist iconography shows, there is still a chance of an encounter. All the individual has to do is shatter in the face of that terror. But this wisdom simply will not do today. In the face of that terror, the West's unified response is to further harden the boundaries of the subjective self by inculcating the wrong kind of knowledge, you know, the kind of knowledge that supports and strengthens the subject-object difference." David added to this, "well, we have even gone past that form of knowledge. Now, the things do not stand out against us as objects, as much as everything has been reshaped as a resource, standing ever ready to be used, and then to be cast aside or made obsolete when no longer useful. The subject-object difference seems to have reached its culmination point in the abstract concept of systems or relations, pure relations, where substantial content no longer is of any concern. You know, your status as an individual self, your comfort, your feelings, your values, are of no relevance to your being a passenger on the plane. All that is necessary is that the seats get filled in the most efficient way to enhance the airline industry in its functioning."

"This point you just made, David, is so important. I think it brings us back to the structure of modern consciousness as being dissociated—something you and I have wrestled with for some time now. On the one hand, in our subjective minds we posit a world of things-as-objects and build a system of knowledge based on that stance—Descartes, as we know. On the other hand we actually conduct our lives or comport ourselves as being in the ontological status of resources, like everything else in the world, and any knowledge born from this side of the configuration remains almost completely mute because it concerns our very *being*, not what we reflect about ourselves."

David said, "somehow, well, we know how, you and I were initiated out of this configuration into another one but it required, as well as the persuasive experience, a decision and we should return to that now." "Ok, where do you want to go next with that?" "Well, we were going on about the central importance of surrender and forgiveness. I think it was you Lisel who conceived of forgiveness as a culmination and transformation of primeval guilt, or as we might put it now, existential anxiety, an apprehension of a primordial state of separation from the Source. So, forgiveness must imply atonement or a reconnection with the Source perhaps in a new way. We both underwent that ordeal and apotheosis, I think." "I agree," said Lisel, "unless" she added ironically, "we're now engaged in a *folie a deux*." "That possibility can surely be tested," said David, "in the field of ordinary reality, which is why we must take all criticism seriously.

"Another aspect of this surrender and forgiveness is the initiate's release from the past. She is no longer bound to the past and her actions are no longer based solely on the past." "In a word," added Lisel, "she is becalmed or one could say, stranded. There is no longer any guidance based on the past or tradition. And yet a decision has to be made if the whole experience is not simply to slide back into oblivion." "It's like Hamlet," Lisel excitedly declared. She had just made an important connection. "Hamlet! He knew what he had to do from the very start. The ghost of his father appeared in the quiet of the garret, which is a suitable image for the psychological state of Hamlet's solitude.

His father informed him about the truth of his death and invoked blood revenge but a decision still had to be made. And Hamlet could not make it. A whole play explores his dreadful uncertainty."

"That's a really interesting analogy," said David. "When you see it in that light, you have to think that Hamlet's consciousness and the correlative world were constituted fundamentally differently from the world when blood consciousness ruled." "Yes, in that latter case," Lisel went on, "there would be no question of whether to take revenge. Blood wisdom *demands* revenge: an eye for an eye, a tooth for a tooth. No questions asked. Decision already made! That is how people still intertwined with Being were instructed and guided by Being and *its* needs, not theirs in any personal sense. It's called the wisdom of the ancestors and it was determinative." David interrupted, "so a key difference in Hamlet lies in his *freedom* to choose, decide." "Yes, it seems he had made his way to a state in which he was becalmed, a state I am now willing to call negative capability, the same state that you and I found ourselves in that night."

"Okay I think we're getting somewhere here, my darling girl. Can we say that if the state of negative capability is achieved, as in Keat's man of achievement, then from that place of silence an image, such as the ghost of Hamlet's father, may appear. The image does not compel because the initiate has achieved a state that is beyond all compulsion, instincts emotions, authority, tradition … " "The image simply, how shall I put it," Lisel completed the thought, "self-presents. It is self-presentational and I think we can go further and say that is the goal of the image that arises from the

Penetralium of Mystery—to self-present!" David went on, "this could go towards the heart of what our free will is really for. We must *freely* choose or not, that is decide or not. And that decision is whether to imitate the self-presenting image in earthly existence through some cultural form or artistic form—which therefore require a redefinition by the way."

"What seems to be at stake in such decision freely made? What is worth dying for, to put it a bit dramatically," asked Lisel. They paused. This was a weighty question. After a time David offered this. "I wonder if it has to do with the whole issue of bringing an aspect of forgotten Being into, how did Heidegger put it, *unconcealment*!" "Oh I think so!" Lisel jumped up. "Yes I believe we're onto something David, right there. We have historically already brought several aspects of Being into unconcealment, the latest one appearing as our entire technological civilization, where the things are showing up as resources to be used and disposed of quite democratically, including us of course. We think that the technological world is the only one, this because we have consigned Being to oblivion. But it is not the only one. You and I know that because we have been reconfigured and the things are beginning to appear to us in a new, quite unexpected way." "You and I," David added, "seem to have begun one of Heidegger's marginal practices." "Let me go on," rushed Lisel, "we in our freedom have consigned Being to oblivion but you know that in principle we're free to do otherwise, but only if the state of negative capability is cultivated, otherwise we're not free, but still compelled by our entanglement in the sensible world. But look, David," Lisel went on, "we have, with varying degrees of consciousness kept Being out by developing systems of knowledge that edify the isolated ego as it holds it's own against the world that is its object of knowledge. But who is stronger, Being, i.e. the Source that that gave us the very freedom to forget it, or us? If Being no longer *wants* to be forgotten, if I can put it that way, and wants to appear in a new form of unconcealment, then it can only do so by impressing upon us it's living intelligence, it's subjectivity, it's *necessity*. And if we meet this ontological necessity with terrified resistance, who will win the day?"

"Or, rather, what cultural forms will emerge from such a high stakes collision of wills," David whispered." Lisel matched him in her quiet tones, " I fear we are already witnessing such forms," she said, "remember Paul Klee …"

AFTERWORD

The very possibility of bringing metaphysics to its turning point ... and turning with it also the way we experience being ... means a critical change in the way thinking unfolds; instead of being guided by conceptual grasp and definition, it is steered and molded by what listening to language discloses, by what insights and avenues it opens. In such changed thinking, what language itself opens up or initiates comes to be amplified in writing so that it quickly acquires a transformative role with regard to thinking, in a way dictating, that is, "saying" its moves and developments.

Afterword

This Afterword, along with the essay in the following chapter, attempts to present a "backstory" to my book. But, like my book, it begins with a dream, an inceptive moment that takes me up in it and begins to "speak through me" although I am quite awake to, and therefore responsible for what I am saying. Dreams are, for me, inceptive moments that lead me into the unknown future. My doctoral program, for example, was founded on a single dream, which continued to unfold and inform me as I went more deeply into my researches. Many of my books had a similar beginning.

And so my Afterword begins with this dream:

I look up and see an awesome display of yellowish turbulence in the sky, lightning forming. I warn others and run for shelter into an old country shop. I see an enormous tree (I see its roots) swirling in the vortex and crash into the rooftops, smashing into the shop.

I wake up. I am no longer running for shelter. There is no tree smashing into rooftops. It's all so normal. And yet, I have a memory of something momentous! Daytime concerns quickly begin to nip at my heels urging me into action, engagement with all the important things. The memory trembles for a moment, sensing the danger of slipping away into oblivion, like so many others. I know a mass suicide of dreams is taking place today, yes suicide— there is a real chance they will not return. I feel the possibility of another victim. I've had so many apocalyptic dreams. And here is another one. I've been writing out of the apocalyptic imagination for decades now. Do I even need to write another one down? The dream memory winces. I feel remorse. Well, I'll write it down. After all, it's my chosen discipline. I've been writing down my dreams for thirty years. One more won't take that much time. Then maybe I can get on with things today.

So, what do we have? A storm, a tree uprooted, and crashing back down. Warning others, running for shelter, O yes, the ol' vortex is back again, and lightning too. Don't forget that!

A silent groan from the depths!

The conscience of my professionalism is then pricked. "You are reading into the dream, my friend. Your interpretation is, so far, quite naturalistic. A tree in the sky must mean an uprooted natural tree. I see! My, my, how much we have learned!"

Ouch! That one hurt!

Chastened, I return to the dream. Ok, the dream did not actually say that. Let's return to the phenomenon and describe it more precisely. It simply shows a tree, roots and leaves, in the vortex, and then crashing into the roof tops. Yes, yes, I know, we even have to be careful about the "in". The dream brings vortex and tree together so I could just as well be describing tree as vortex, or vortex as tree. There is a unity and a difference being shown here, in picture form. Vortex and tree somehow belong together in their difference.

Now I begin to realize my abysmal ignorance. Did I just hear a sigh of relief emanating from somewhere—the abyss? Time to set to work, this time the real work! I will not be an accomplice to one more suicide.

Tree, trees in the air, that's not so wildly alien to the human experience. The alchemical tree, the philosopher's tree, the inverted tree with its roots in heaven and branches touching the earth! This tree exists as a property of the mind and is no less real for that. I'll begin my researches there.

Don't worry dream. I will not forget you now. I'll be back, soon. I just have to catch up with what you are already saying, yes *saying.* Another memory comes. This time I know that it, too, belongs to the gathering nest of images attracted to my dream memory:

What ultimately bestows the material for the new style is the style of a people's language. Art takes place in the clearing "which has already happened and unnoticed in language."[1] Heidegger goes on to remind us about the nature of art today:

Art, as the setting-into-work of truth, is poetry. Not only the creation of the work is poetic, but equally poetic, though in its own way, is the preserving of the work; for a work is in actual effect as a work only when we remove ourselves from our commonplace routine and move into what is disclosed by the work, so is to bring our own nature itself to take a stand in the truth of what is.[2]

The "new style" or new paradigm thus begins with a bestowal. A new cultural configuration, or new understanding of being is founded "in the clearing" in a momentous inception. When Heidegger speaks of this *happening* in terms of language, he means that a bestowal can only take place from within the "past", i.e. our given tradition of language. It must therefore appear almost incomprehensible, yet somehow intelligible, just as my tree-vortex appears.

My dream is a self-presentation of a saying. The figures comprising it are figures of speech. I am being

spoken to, addressed, by language and it is truth! Now I
recall that tree and truth both spring from a common
etymological root—*deru-*, which carries a meaning of
firmness, solidity, steadfastness, just the qualities one
would want in trees and truth.

Now another memory comes to the fore—vortices. I
have spent a lot of time with vortices. One even became
the central character in another book I wrote: *UR-image*!
During my research I discovered that "vortex" or "spiral"
is closely related to a form of speech. One could even talk
of spirallic speech, as I do in this subsequent book,
Oblivion of Being. This sense of "turning" is central to
Heidegger's thought (in his Contributions to Philosophy)
of the "event", that originary clearing whose primary
quality is *silence*: "Every language of Da-sein originates here
and is thus in essence silence (c.f. restraint, event, truth,
and language) … The event has its innermost occurrence
and its furthest reach *in the turning* [which is] the intrusion
of beying [the originary language]."

Heidegger is telling us that there are several aspects to
the artistic effort today. First he is telling us that the
location of the artistic effort is in the "clearing". This
clearing is found when the artist removes himself from his
commonplace routine and takes a stand in the truth of
what it is. Only then, you might say, does the human
participant *become* the artist, ready to receive and produce
the truth of what is, as it is bestowed. I received my dream
in such a clearing, which must be "prior" to my
subsequent waking up with the dream-as-memory, once
again in that normal mode of consciousness called *reflective*.

The preserving of the work is another aspect of the
creative act. I take this to mean that, although the work is
done in the clearing, in the receiving and production of

"what has already happened and unnoticed in language", an art form is produced, preserving the inceptive moment. This "preserving" is what I am doing right now, as this essay, and as my book.

With these amplifications now swirling in the vortex, along with my dream tree, I can return to my dream memory with renewed purpose. Yes, the dream is saying something, something I must hear, a truth. Can I get closer to that clearing in my waking life? Can I be sufficiently open to the unknown? Truth, trees! I know that for Plato and for generations after him, down to the present time, truth was indeed in the sky: the Forms— eternal truths, beyond the world of the senses. The world of our routine lives, and art, were secondary to these truths—belonging to contingency, the apparent. No truth to be found here. Human being was pictured as a tree, an inverted tree with its roots in heaven and its branches touching the earth. Wolfgang Giegerich tells us the meaning of this strange and compelling symbol, following on from Jung's researches into the Philosophical Tree:

When the Song of Songs, Ovid, the medieval Minnesingers, Petrarch, Shakespeare, and so on express feelings of love, we must not retrojectively read their poems as their self-expression, their personal feelings "coming from their inner," as if they had already been modern individuals. Their poems—and the love feelings articulated in them—are essentially literature. The articulation of those feelings occurred as literary events. They were revolutionary inventions and productions, discoveries at the very forefront of cultural development. Anticipations. The feelings were born "above" and "outside of" the poets as literal persons; they first appeared in and as those literary texts, in and as words, in and as the poetic rhetorical phrases, images, and metaphors they found, not in the person or psyche (let alone "the unconscious") of their authors. The possibility to articulate these feelings as poets did not at all mean that they as human beings, as "civil men (or women)," would already have been capable of actually having such feelings as subjective emotions. The place of where "the real action was," of where the true life of people was lived, was up there, in what was above the heads, above people's practical reality. We remember: man is (or at least was) an "arbor inversa," a tree that has its roots in the sky and its treetops in the earth.[3]

In reading this profound passage I was particularly struck by one sentence, "we remember: man is (or at least was) an 'arbor inversa,' a tree that has its roots in the sky and treetops in earth." Giegerich wrote in brackets, almost in passing, "*or at least was*". The essence of Man *was* an "arbor inversa"—*was*! What can this mean? And if it is true then what is the essence of Man now?

Giegerich goes on to address this question. He describes how truth, the Forms, lost their potency correlatively with a growing emphasis on the centrality of the individual, i.e. the being who now *bestows* meaning *on* an otherwise inert world, overcoming the former being who *received* meaning *from* the world:

[I]deas and concepts have lost their former status of ultimate realness as "universals" in the neoplatonic sense, a realness superior to that of the particular and the concrete individual who had formerly only possessed reality to the extent that he *participated* in and was subsumed under the universal. ...
Today, what actually occurs in individuals in all their diversity *is* the only real, and ideas, concepts, roles are seen as no more than human constructs. The singular has emancipated itself from the universal concept, which is now in fact reduced to a *flatus vocis* or experienced as a mere human instrument of oppression.[4]

In response to another memory that suddenly intruded, I quickly turned to Jung's book *Alchemical Studies*, to the section on the inverted tree, where my eyes were immediately riveted to a passage quoted by Jung:

The roots of its ores are in the air and the summits in the earth. And when they are torn from their places, a terrible sound is heard and there follows a great fear.[5]

Jung quoted this short passage as an amplification of his theme of the inverted tree but he does not tell us what the old alchemist had in mind when he wrote such a strange thing. Why would he be talking about the inverted tree being torn from its place? Was it not secure? Was there already in the 16th century some intimation of a catastrophic happening, a catastrophe of truth and the essence of man? This passage was written at the time of Descartes who articulated, for the first time, the possibility of the essence of Man as the being who no longer simply receives reality and its gifts of bestowal (such as poetry). He can now *represent* reality, *posit* those representations as *the* new reality, and thus manipulate it to his own ends. A rupture was thus created between former Being and representation which was now posited as the new Being. Now the former Being was only real to the extent that it could be represented, otherwise it was to be forgotten.

The oblivion of former true Being had begun in earnest!

Was the old alchemist sensing this impending rupture in his compelling image of the *arbor inversa* torn from its place? Where it formerly held the status of true Being, it is now in the status of being represented, i.e. it has been torn from its original place in Heaven and now appears in Man's representations—a ghostly reflection of its former glory.

Is my dream in some way related to *this* catastrophe, the oblivion of "original" Being? I am using this word, "catastrophe" several times. What is trying to get through here, in this speech? I open the dictionary and find images of turning, like the vortex, or whirlwind, with the added inflection of turning down, ruination, conclusion, and most surprisingly, buried deep with the root *cat-*, lies a meaning of giving birth in the sense that many animals give birth standing up, dropping their young to the ground.

The unknown future is concealed within these tiny, unnoticed details of our (linguistic) past—what Heidegger calls "marginal practices"—that have been sidelined by the dominant paradigm, or cultural prejudice. Any one of these marginal practices can, at any time, become the seed of a new configuration of Being, leading to, in effect, a new world of appearances. The "artist" is the one who can bring such marginal practices forth into actuality.

I was attracted to this tiny detail of a birth, taking place within a catastrophe. There was yet another unexpected detail that also caught my eye, this time in relation to the root *streb(h)-*. In amongst images of spiraling, going down, vortices, turning, twisting, winding, is a Greek word *strabos*, which means "squinting". How can squinting belong to this nest of meanings?

I decided to follow this thread and next looked up the word "squint". There, among the usual meanings of looking askance, closing the eyes while partly looking, etc., is a meaning that leaped out at me: to squint is to have an indirect or oblique reference or inclination. During the course of the evolution of language, an outer meaning had inverted to mean an inner or psychological disposition.

Apparently, my dream, in the form of a tree-vortex, is saying a kind of truth-speech that is expressed in a spirallic form with a quality of indirection, oblique reference. It occurs in a mood of turbulence, chaos, catastrophe, but also, as my dream says, lightning, i.e. inception, bringing a new configuration of Being into sudden appearance, a new birth, a new definition of what it is to be human.

Nietzsche *said* this catastrophe, *lived* this catastrophe! He said what has "already happened and unnoticed in language" over a period of 2500 years. The truth, or the former true world of ideal forms, has emptied out, become an idol, *living logos* become *flatus vocis*, leaving what Heidegger calls a "vacant niche", or Nietzsche's "fiction":

We have done away with the true world: what world is left over? The apparent one, maybe? ... But no! *Along with the true world, we have also done away with the apparent!* [6]

This quote is the 6th aphorism from the chapter: How the "True World" Finally Became a Fiction". The true world become a fiction! Something deep in me simply says, yes! Read this well! Everything that was understood to be the ultimate reality and truth, from Plato's forms, down to Christian metaphysics—i.e. the true world, has now become a fiction, an error. The ideal-apparent duality of eternal forms and contingency has finally been demolished. What is left? An error, yes, but there is more—a new birth. Nietzsche goes on:

(Midday; moment of the shortest shadow; end of the longest error; high point of humanity; INCIPIT ZARATHUSTRA.)

A new birth on Earth—now the true world—and it is bestowed on us as "already happened and unnoticed in language." But how is this new true world configured? What are its contours? And what kind of human being is able to perceive these contours? How can it be *spoken*?

My dream shows what *was* the true world, but is now a fiction, an error, crashing into the rooftops where I am sheltered. How was I to know that "shelter" also derives from *deru-*, the very root of truth and tree? Is the former true world, downgraded by history to fiction, now being sheltered here, on earth in the ordinary world that was formerly felt to be absent of truth in its contingency and instability, hardly enduring? How can the contingent and changing be simultaneously stable and enduring? Surely we are here approaching Nietzsche's meaning of the *eternal recurrence of the same*!

Heidegger was intensely interested in such questions too. He notes how Nietzsche's cry of "God is dead" points to an overturning or abolition of Platonism with its ontological oppositional structure of the supersensuous or "true world" and the sensuous or "apparent world", along with a transformation in the definition of what it is to be human:

[T]he overturning of Platonism and the ultimate twist out of it imply a metamorphosis of man. At the end of Platonism stands a decision concerning the transformation of man ... whether he is to become that kind of man Nietzsche characterized as the "last man," or whether that type of man can be overcome and the "overman" can begin: "Incipit Zarathustra."

With the abolition of Platonism the way first opens for the affirmation of the sensual, and along with it the non-sensuous world of the spirit as well.[7]

Heidegger then reminds us of Nietzsche's own words from *Will to Power*:

I wish an ever-greater spiritualization and augmentation of the senses. Yes, we ought to be grateful to our senses for their subtlety, fullness, and force; and we ought to offer them in return the very best of spirit we possess.[8]

Heidegger claims that what is needed is not an abolition of the sensuous nor abolition of the non-sensuous, for that would be an ultimate nihilism. Instead, a path must be cleared for a new interpretation of the sensuous on the basis of a new ordering structure of the sensuous and non-sensuous. Life must now be interpreted on the basis of Being:

The equation of Being and life … [is a] a transformed interpretation of the biological on the basis of Being, grasped in a superior way, this of course not fully mastered, in the timeworn schema of "Being and Becoming." … "Overman" is the man who grounds Being anew in the rigor of knowledge and in the grand style of creation.[9]

"Not fully mastered!" I am reminded of Giegerich who adds this cautionary note to such aspirations or, as he says, utopian schemes:

Both the diagnosis of the loss of meaning and the idea of the dire need of meaning … are nothing new. They had already been experienced and struggled with in different ways for at least one hundred years prior to Jung. The 19th century had not only discovered what was to become known under the catchword "nihilism," defined by Nietzsche as the lack of a goal, the lack of an answer to the "What for?"; it had also desperately tried, in ever new utopian schemes, to provide a new, ultimate goal of life. To mention only three examples, Kierkegaard had proposed a leap into faith, Marx had promised the communist society, and Nietzsche had put all his hope onto the longed for advent of what he imaged under the symbolic name "Dionysus," who would come to and inspire "Ariadne," the deserted soul ready to receive Dionysus, thereby ending the sterility reached in the 19th century ... None of these had had enough power of conviction to lastingly bind the collective mind, and especially after Nietzsche's collapse due to his realization that his expectation [of the "overman"] would and could not come true, the lesson of the 19th century about the untenableness of utopias had been learned.[10]

Giegerich's statement here arises in the context of an essay called "The End of Meaning and the Birth of Man." His purpose is to show how nihilism is not a problem to be solved, but a new way of being that had come into dominance during the 19th century—one that we can simply get used to, or not:

This loss [of meaning—my insert] is not an interlude. It makes a *real* difference. But rather than inflating man into an overman, it forces man in his concept of himself to come down from his former lofty height and to live *without* being dressed in any splendid religious or mythical garments.[11]

Giegerich's overall project is to show how 2500 years of the *reflective mind*'s historical development has now drawn to a close with the attainment of what he calls *absolute* interiority—a state of mind that reflectingly knows itself *as a self*, as pure mindedness, what he calls the living concept, "I". This logical structure has been reached by the soul and our culture is slowly working its way to that realization as reflected in modern cultural practices that articulate its reality and truth.

So, whatever the "overman" may offer it cannot relieve each of us of the responsibility of coming to terms with our ordinariness (no mythic garments). Seeking refuge in a new meaning that can hold us, embrace us, or surround us, is utopian and doomed to failure, as Giegerich says. Throughout his works, he, too, recognizes a momentous soul event that occurs around the 19th century, expressed as a transformation from a determinative "vertical" (eternity-*saeculum*) sense of time to an historical (past-future) one.

Giegerich thus understands the "world-shaking" event of a "coming down to earth" as a mooring of the soul in the temporal world as the past-future guiding difference, opening up the possibility of *historical* consciousness—a further development in the complexity of the reflective mind: it now has the capacity to reflect on itself *historically*.

There is a long philosophical tradition backing Giegerich's claims regarding the reflective mind's coming home to itself in absolute interiority. For example, he discusses Hegel's concern with "real knowledge" and "insight" by which he means "science" in its rational character:

The impulse driving [Hegel's] work is clearly counter to any type of self-expression or any offering himself as the passive mouthpiece of a "self-revelation of the psychic background."

Such activities (i.e. revelations or bringing forth ultimate truths of that kind) are pointless "because they have long since been available in catechisms or popular sayings."[12]

Hegel's startling claim (in which Giegerich finds a philosophical basis for in his own work) can be best understood as being true only of the memory, or reproductive imagination (what I call the reflective mind), but certainly not of the productive imagination, which deals with the very "anticipations" that Giegerich earlier spoke of in relation to the production of poetry.

The job of philosophy, according to Giegerich's Hegel, is only to work out the Concept or Notion, i.e. the conceptual knowledge of what there is to be known, the careful rational account of the real. Giegerich even includes Hegel's derisive and scornful attitude towards anything to do to with "revelations", "oracles" etc. at least as far as philosophy is concerned:

… human nature only really exists in an *achieved* [my italics] community of minds. The anti-human, the merely animal, consists in staying in the sphere of feeling, and being able to communicate only at the level ... the man of common sense makes his appeal to feeling, to an oracle within his breast.[13]

Giegerich's Hegel privileges philosophy as "the careful account of the real", the worked out Concept or Notion, the conceptual knowledge of what there is to be known, i.e. the domain of the reflective mind and its forms of knowing!

It seems to me that this view of philosophy is irreconcilable with Heidegger's view, as expressed in the Contributions, and his later work on inceptive thinking etc. Heidegger's project was to recover the former true Being from oblivion. He felt that the kind of philosophy that Hegel privileged, based as it was on man as rational animal, or as I have described it, reflective or representational consciousness, continues the Western path of ensuring the oblivion of the former true Being, as it completes its telos of *absolute* interiority (reflection).

Polt puts it this way:

Ordinarily, to think is to **represent** entities ... [but] inceptive thinking is marked by its attention to the hidden and possible *as such*, by its distrust of all efforts to **represent** [my emphasis] the inceptive event, and by its ambition to *participate* in the event, not simply to observe it.[14]

Heidegger is trying to rethink philosophy altogether so that it can adequately carry the inceptive moment, not merely capture, in thought, what has already been (Hegel's "careful account of the real"). "Could it be", asks Polt:

that [philosophy] must become *futural thinking*, opening possibilities instead of describing givens? ... Philosophy has almost always been written in the present tense and indicative mood—but might there be a future-subjunctive philosophy?[15]

He goes on:

We could argue that poets hope for a similar shift. The goal of poetry is to rejuvenate and transform our ways of perceiving what is—in other words, to participate in and even "found" the emergence of meaning, the event of be-ing ... Poetry opens new prospects. But philosophy typically takes a retrospective position, summing up the sense of all that has unfolded ... Philosophy may begin with wonder, but it tries to replace wonder with understanding (Aristotle, Met. A 2). The owl of Minerva spreads its wings only at dusk (Hegel, *Philosophy of Right*, Preface). But these thoughts will not apply perfectly to Heidegger. He is quite capable of structured and synoptic thought, and we will see that the *Contributions*, tentative and fragmentary as they are, do form a kind of whole. But he does not want bethinking to be retrospective—in fact, we have seen that it itself is a possibility at least as much as an activity. Bethinking must be *inceptive* thinking.[16]

The language is hypnotically repetitive and dense, consisting of formula after formula in which Heidegger tries to say everything unsayable all at once … As an account of the "essential happening of be-ing," the text resembles a treatise; as an investigation of the roots of concepts, it resembles history of philosophy; as an analysis of a crisis, it resembles cultural critique; as an invocation of a moment of decision, it resembles prophecy; as a self-conscious deployment of language, it resembles poetry … [17]

I now have this philosophical backstory firmly in mind as I return to my dream. How can these important considerations relate to my dream's *saying*?

Thoughts, images, are swirling, chaotic. I must pay attention to whatever presents itself to me, but I must do so without undue grasping, i.e. without trying to make sense of it all by reducing the chaos back to the familiar. It's too big a storm. Many minds have been broken by it, including, it seems, Nietzsche's.

One connection, however, *has* been made and it seems to endure. It feels strangely stable amid the swirling chaos: Nietzsche's *Twilight of the Idols*! His chapter entitled, "How the 'True World' Finally Became a Fiction" connects somehow with my dream image of the sky tree crashing into the rooftops as well as with my own researches leading up to the dream. I think I may have finally succeeded, with the help of my dream, in making explicit the relationship between my own work into the interpenetration of fictional and empirical realities, new genres of literature, and the deeper context of the history of Being, as represented in the work of Nietzsche and Heidegger.

Let me try to *say* it…

The tree crashes into the rooftops. Is it seeking shelter there? The "true world" has become an error, a vacant niche, under the 2000 yearlong event of nihilism.

What can a penetration of the fictional (past truth), into the empirical possibly mean? If, as Heidegger says, "art takes place in the clearing which has already happened and unnoticed in language," then my dream is pointing to a momentous event in language. Former true Being, in oblivion for over 2000 years—reduced in ontological status from truth to fiction, or error; concepts, *logos*, Forms, emptied out of their former status as ultimate reality and now merely instruments of human communication or exploitation—now having catastrophically interpenetrated with ordinary, empirical reality, perhaps even seeking shelter there, in Heidegger's sense that beings may shelter Being:

Beings may no longer be taken for granted as present-at-hand things [i.e. the objects of a reflective consciousness—my insert], but will be experienced as sheltering the inexhaustible truth of be-ing that is simultaneous with them.[18]

Our current world of present-at-hand things is a world devoid of depth, meaning, infinity, as we know. Prior to the 19th century the perceived and experienced world of human beings was (or could become) symbolic or imaginal. The world of things was still grounded in the infinite depths of the psyche, and at any time that depth could reveal itself to us, as reflected in the things of the world. Thus the things could, at times, still "speak" to us. Around the time of the Industrial Revolution, this ground disappeared completely, leaving us in a perceived world of surface only, with no depth (i.e., intelligence, wisdom, infinity, subjectivity, etc.) at all. This was also the time in which personhood was invented—Heidegger's world of Dasein. It was and remains a world of "poverty of symbols", where the previous symbol-bearing things of the world (Heidegger's "things") have become mere resources—including us!

Wolfgang Giegerich compares the time when the things still had their own depth, mystery, and "inexhaustible truth", with our modern world:

The once infinite bottomless expanse of the wild, to which human existence was exposed and in which it was completely contained ... has been narrowed down to a finite positive thing, an empirical object, a particular ... when once it had been a *topos*, a world, the world of terror. And this terror has been taken away from the real ravine; it has ceased being an objective quality of reality—ontological, cosmological, or mythical—and turned into a mere human feeling, a subjective state in man ... Here we can witness the transition from an existence grounded in the imagination to an existence in positivism ... [19]

If it is Being that gives depth, meaning, inexhaustible truth, my dream as an event of language, suggests very strongly that the language of beings today as reflected in a world of positivity is now being opened up to an infinite world of meaning interpenetrating with it. Such an inception or event would produce a most startling and bewildering form of language or what I would call, genre of literature. I have already mentioned Heidegger's Contributions to Philosophy as a form of literature that has attracted vigorous and contentious secondary scholarship, as did Nietzsche's entire body of dithyrambic work when it was first published. But where else may we look today to find hints, suggestions, anticipations, of a modern form of literature or style of language that is sheltering the former true Being as depth, meaning, truth, "within" it?

The birth of this new genre, if my dream portends it, must have the character or mood of a catastrophe of inceptive language crashing into and being sheltered by "tradition" perhaps in the sense that Polt means:

What if we could discover events of appropriation, inceptions, and emergency at work even within the ordinary, even in the realm of reproducibility? ... One would have to use living language in combination with precise vocabulary.[20]

Polt's "one would have to use ..." needs to be qualified though. If we are talking about former true Being interpenetrating with ordinary empirical life today, then the empirical person in some sense would become the "clearing" in which the inceptive moment takes place. The empirical person would need to be the shelter for the entire catastrophic event. It would not be enough simply to write imaginatively about such an event. The event would be happening as the writing happens (or art, or some other medium) and it would be as Polt suggests, "a living language in combination with precise vocabulary", or "arranging marriages between inherited words and inceptive moments."

Who is writing this way today?

I have been in the grip of this question for several decades. I personally endured my version of the "catastrophic event" and began to write in a way that I could not fathom, but, at first, was driven to do so. In one of my early attempts to articulate the form of writing I was doing, I wrote:

I begin by paying attention to certain events occurring in the world: i.e. events characterized by qualities of the unusual, the unfamiliar, the startling all of which obviously involve my psychological participation, and then I open myself up to these phenomena sufficiently for them to penetrate my consciousness, so that I begin to think the thought of the phenomenon, distinct from my thinking about them This process is in effect an initiation into another form of consciousness, the consciousness of the phenomenon. This finally can form the basis for new action in the world, action that is not simply a repeat of the known past but instead carries the germ of a new future. These actions always took me away from the security of the familiar into the unknown future.

My method of writing is therefore an attempt to develop an art form that can demonstrate this process. I soften the boundaries of my ego and pay attention to unusual, unfamiliar, or even startling images that "arrive". I take up a relationship with these visitors and am prepared to leave my present path to follow their hints. I record this process as it goes on. A kind of wandering therefore takes place in my writing as in my life ...

In this way, I move from a memory, to a dream, to a reflection of an event in the world, to an etymological study of a word, to the words of another author. I do not concern myself with any separation between inner and outer, past and future, fact and fiction i.e. the usual categories of experience. The one constant is that all my writing springs out of the soil of immediate experience and so is real. I pay attention to detail, or hints that emerge freely from "within", no matter how small or seemingly insignificant. It takes a kind of surrender to psychic process in order to write this way, and a faith that I won't fall merely into chaos, or madness. But this is far from certain!

In order to ground my work, I cast a net out into the community of ideas, in order to find other souls who were faced with same perplexing form of writing/consciousness. My books are all attempts to embed my own work in a community of souls who were likewise attempting the form of writing that Polt describes as, "a living language in combination with precise vocabulary." As I did so, my understanding distilled, or refined, until, in 2014, I was able to give my clearest articulation by reference to C. G. Jung's Liber Novis, or, The Red Book:

The Red Book is an account of a momentous achievement by Jung—an achievement that I have called his hidden legacy. During the course of his ordeal, Jung found his way to the mode of being that Heidegger calls a clearing, where a new world can appear, as languaged in the polyphonic form that the editors of The Red Book rendered so faithfully for us. This clearing is also a new definition of the human being, one which can "welcome the coming guest", with a new soul capacity to be the new language—language which, to our present form of consciousness, appears "life- threatening," mad, and abyssal— the end of the world![21]

The following chapter contains my complete essay on the *form* of The Red Book, as an example of an emerging genre of literature, the language of which "shelters", once again, the immeasurable depths of Being. My hope is that both my book, its Afterword, and this essay will further deepen our understanding of what is at stake in the human being's willingness to become a "clearing" that can allow, after 2500 years of oblivion, Being to speak at last.

But before we enter that essay, and in order to prepare us for it, perhaps, let us hear two examples of likely linguistic precursors. One occurs in Jung's life, prior to his engagement with the material that constitutes The Red Book.[22] It is a sustained event that carries exactly the phenomenology of an inceptive "moment" in which "a precise vocabulary" begins to shelter poetic or "living language", generating a new linguistic form. The following account is given by Kerr and refers to the mysterious encounter between Jung and Sabina Spielrein:

The secret meetings had been about poetry. They had been about the strange turn of imagination that can arise when a sexual attraction asserts itself. As Spielrein put it, "we could sit in speechless ecstasy for hours". But, we do well to understand that this imaginative turn was likely given a psychoanalytic cast as well … Spielrein regularly identified Jung with both her father and her younger brother … while Jung regularly identified her with his mother. These identifications I would suggest, not only constituted an interpretation of their shared Siegfried fantasy but also sometimes alternated with it in the rapture of their mutual enchantment. Interpretation had been a prelude to fantasy and both, by degrees, had begun to blend with lived experience …

In short, poetry was Spielrein's word for what happens when a couple, both enamored of mysticism, move backward from it to a sexual realization—and keep psychoanalysing. Analysis and fantasy, incest and myth, had started to merge into each other. Freud may certainly be excused by history if he failed to grasp what the young woman was going on about.[23]

The second equally compelling example is an account
given by Nietzsche (as quoted by his sister) of the
phenomenology of inspiration, with particular reference to
his writing Zarathustra:

One hears—one does not seek; one takes—one does not ask
who gives: a thought suddenly flashes up like lightning, it comes
with necessity, unhesitatingly—I have never had any choice in
the matter. There is an ecstasy such that the immense strain of it
is sometimes relaxed by a flood of tears, along with which one's
steps either rush or involuntarily lag, alternately. There is the
feeling that one is completely out of hand, with the very distinct
consciousness of an endless number of fine thrills and
quiverings to the very toes;—there is a depth of happiness in
which the painfullest and gloomiest do not operate as antitheses,
but as conditioned, as demanded in the sense of necessary
shades of colour in such an overflow of light ... Everything
happens quite involuntarily, as if in a tempestuous outburst of
freedom, of absoluteness, of power and divinity. The
involuntariness of the figures and similes is the most remarkable
thing; one loses all perception of what constitutes the figure and
what constitutes the simile; everything seems to present itself as
the readiest, the correctest and the simplest means of
expression. It actually seems, to use one of Zarathustra's own
phrases, as if all things came unto one, and would fain be
similes: 'Here do all things come caressingly to thy talk and
flatter thee, for they want to ride upon thy back. On every simile
dost thou here ride to every truth. Here fly open unto thee all
being's words and word-cabinets; here all being wanteth to
become words, here all becoming wanteth to learn of thee how
to talk.'[24]

ENDNOTES

1. Dreyfus, H. (2005). "Heidegger's Ontology of Art". *A Companion to Heidegger.* (Kindle; location 7495).
2. Heidegger, M. (1971). *Poetry, Language, Thought.* New York. Harper Colophon books. P. 74-75.
3. Giegerich, W. (2012). *What is Soul?* New Orleans. Spring Journal Books. P. 178.
4. Giegerich, W. (2010). *The Soul Always Thinks.* New Orleans. Spring Journal Books. P. 200.
5. Jung, C. G. (1976). *Alchemical Studies.* Princeton. Princeton University Press. P. 311.
6. Nietzsche, F. (1997). *Twilight of the Idols.* Indianapolis. Hackett Publishing Co. Inc.
7. Heidegger, M. (1979). "The Will to Power as Art". *Nietzsche.* San Francisco. Harper and Row. Pp. 208-
8. Ibid.
9. Ibid. Pp. 219-20.
10. Giegerich, W. (2010). "The End of Meaning and the Birth of Man". *The Soul Always Thinks.* Op. Cit. Pp. 190-1; 240.
11. Ibid. P. 209
12. Giegerich, W. (2013). *C. G. Jung on Christianity and on Hegel. Part 2.* New Orleans. Spring Journal Books. Pp. 332.
13. Hegel, as quoted by Giegerich. Ibid. P. 330.
14. Polt, R. (2004). *The Emergency of Being: On Heidegger's Contributions to Philosophy.* Ithaca. Cornell University Press. Pp. 88 & 104.
15. Ibid. P. 98.
16. Ibid. Pp. 114-5.
17. Ibid. P. 2.
18. Ibid. P. 194.
19. Giegerich, W. (2007). *Technology and the Soul.* New Orleans. Spring Journal Books. P. 33.
20. Polt, R. (2004). *The Emergency of Being: On Heidegger's Contributions to Philosophy.* Ithaca. Cornell University Press. Pp. 182-3.

21. Excerpt from next chapter.
22. First published in: Thomas Arzt (Hrsg.): *Das Rote Buch. C. G. Jungs Reise zum "anderen Pol der Welt" Studien zur Analytischen Psychologie, Bd. 5*, Königshausen & Neumann, Würzburg, Germany, 2015.
23. Kerr, J. (1994). *A Most Dangerous Method: The Story of Jung, Freud, and Sabina Spielrein.* New York. Vintage Books. Pp. 226-7.
24. Nietzsche, F. (1905). *Thus Spake Zarathustra.* From the Introduction.

HIDDEN LEGACY OF THE RED BOOK

[C]ontents of the unconscious [are] in statu nascendi, in the state of being born. They are suspended, they are in the labor pains of birth, and the creative consciousness is identified with that condition. Therefore the creator will put himself into that state of suspension, of torment, in order to embody or incarnate the unconscious contents ... So the suspended ideas which should reach the daylight, can only appear when one takes away from the other side—the side of the body— so that the idea can produce a body to appear in for itself. The idea is like an autonomous being that wants a body so much that it even incarnates in the body: one begins to play, to perform the idea, and then people say one is completely mad ... Such a state, then, is necessarily followed by a certain product. C. G. Jung (Zarathustra Seminars, 194, 197)

INTRODUCTION: Interpretation of Texts

There are many ways to interpret even the simplest text, each way being backed by the interpreter's discipline and corresponding methodology, and as we have learned from Gadamer, by the "effective history" informing and guiding the consciousness and "possibilities of knowing" of the interpreter.[1] In approaching a book as rich and complex as The Red Book, therefore, I think it is crucial, as far as possible, for the interpreter to acknowledge, from the outset, the "discipline", "methodology" and "effective history" that are informing his effort of interpretation so as to declare his prejudices and limitations.

In this essay, I am guided by a few key notions that Gadamer's philosophical hermeneutics bring forward, as he asks:

[w]hat it is that really makes the productive scholar. That he has learned the methods? The person who never produces anything new has also done that. It is imagination [Phantasie] that is the decisive function of the scholar. Imagination naturally has a hermeneutical function and serves the sense for what is questionable. It serves the ability to expose real, productive questions, something in which, generally speaking, only he who masters all the methods of his science succeeds.[2]

Gadamer elsewhere describes the exposure of "real, productive questions", as a hermeneutical event:

[T]he hermeneutical event proper is not language as language, whether as grammar or as lexicon; it consists in the coming into language of what has been said in the tradition: an event that is at once appropriation and interpretation.

Thus here it really is true to say that this event is not our action upon the thing, but the act of the thing itself.[3]

Beistegui gives us an example of a hermeneutical event, or experience, in the sense that Gadamer understands, with reference to Heidegger's masterful interpretation of Greek texts:

Most striking, then, was Heidegger's ability to see Aristotle not as a historically important object, but as a way of clarifying the most pressing and urgent question of the time, namely, that of life.

In his writings, and more so even in his teaching, Heidegger was able to make the Greeks speak as if for the first time by anchoring their thought in the fundamental experiences of human existence. His phenomenological and hermeneutical approach brought the canonical Greek texts back to life by bringing them back into the concrete life-world of our own experience (the "factical life") ... Heidegger's students had the impression that the Greeks were speaking to them directly across the ages, and that the questions of the Greeks were – or had become – their own. This, in effect, was the source of what Gadamer [who was there] called the 'fundamental hermeneutic experience', which became the focus of his own philosophy.[4]

A fundamental hermeneutic experience that clarifies the most pressing and urgent question of the time! This is the way that The Red Book spoke to me when I opened its pages after attending the inaugural seminar on The Red Book in Zurich in 2009. This essay, then, is an attempt to articulate how my experience of The Red Book further clarifies the most pressing and urgent question of our time. I will proceed by way of asking how Jung began to conceive and articulate this question. Following this discussion, I will present a brief self-disclosure of my own encounter with the question of our times in order to show how The Red Book further clarified that question for me and, following the hermeneutic circle, I will then re-enter the text of The Red Book in order to illuminate the text in the light of my conception of the question.

THE PRESSING and URGENT QUESTION of OUR TIMES

In 2008, Wolfgang Giegerich presented a lecture at the Jung Institute Zürich entitled, C. G. Jung's Psychology Project as a Response to the Condition of the World.[5] Giegerich begins by examining what Jung meant when he said in 1960, "those who mouth my name have fundamentally no idea of what it is all about."[6] Giegerich shows that what Jung means is something existential, "an enormous problem that we today are confronted with"—the condition of the world, as the title of the lecture says. Much of the lecture is then devoted to what possible meaning of "world" Jung is so concerned with when he claims, for example: "The great problem of our time is that we don't understand what is happening to the world."[7]

While there are many available notions of world, Giegerich sharply distinguishes Jung's notion from the "popular one that makes headlines" i.e., the positive-factual world of global warming, population explosion, diminishing resources, etc. The condition of the world that Jung is addressing "remains unseen and not understood, indeed—so Jung felt—suppressed out of fear."[8] Giegerich then goes on to untangle some confusion in Jung's own thinking regarding the meaning of his notion of world before bringing us to his interpretation of Jung's understanding of world— the understanding that, according to Giegerich, led Jung to make his startling claim that "the great problem of our time is that we don't understand what is happening to the world". Giegerich says this world is:

[T]hat world whose existence depends on two sources, its being and its being known. I mean the world of man that is perceived and experienced and that speaks—speaks not only through literal symbols, but also through and in all the diverse human responses given to it.[9]

Having established, through argument, the notion of world that Jung was fundamentally concerned with throughout his life, Giegerich proceeds to ask what Jung saw as happening to the world, or, what was/is the condition of the world which addressed Jung throughout his life as the pressing and urgent question (or truth) of our time:

[Jung] not only factually lived in the truth of his age, as all people inevitably do, but like other great, exceptional minds he was also open to it, was reached by it and himself reached with his soul's root-fibers into the truth of the collective situation."[10]

The rest of Giegerich's lecture addresses Jung's understanding of (and his response to) the truth of our times, beginning with a plethora of quotes taken from Jung's works, on the way to his (Giegerich's) summation:

There is an absolute rupture in history, a fundamental crisis in the singular. This crisis separates "all ages before us" from us and our time. The situation we find ourselves in is absolutely unparalleled. …[11]

[W]hat Jung envisioned is a fundamental collapse of the entire reality level itself from its previous high level, the level of religion and metaphysics as great externally existing forms, to the fundamentally lower level of psychology and its immediate confrontation with the unconscious.[12]

I will leave Giegerich's essay here, i.e., with his interpretation of Jung's diagnosis of the condition of the world today, having specified the notion of world that Jung was so concerned with and his consequent conception of the pressing and urgent question of our time (or the truth of our times).

The condition of the world at the time of Jung's embarking on The Red Book is described, in its positive-factual features, by Shamdasani, in a citation from 1913:

The world and society in 1913 looked like this: life is completely confined and shackled. A kind of economic fatalism prevails: each individual, whether he resists it or not, is assigned a specific role and with it his interests and his character. The church is regarded as a "redemption factory" of little importance, literature as a safety valve … The most burning question day and night is: is there anywhere a force that is strong enough to put an end to this state of affairs? And if not, how can one escape it?[13]

When Jung was only twelve years old he was initiated into the truth of this emerging world, as the metaphysical ground of a previous world underwent its fundamental collapse, corresponding to "the end of existence in the paradise of childhood, in 'God's world'."[14]

Shamdasani goes on to assert that, "[w]ithin this cultural crisis, Jung conceived of undertaking an extended process of self-experimentation, which resulted in Liber Novus, a work of psychology in a literary form."[15]

Thanks to Shamdasani's ground-breaking research, The Red Book is now generally interpreted as constituting "the bedrock and foundation"[16] of Jung's future psychology project—in agreement with Jung's own assessment:

It has taken me virtually forty-five years to distill within the vessel of my scientific work the things I experienced and wrote down at that time [i.e., The Red Book—my insert]. As a young man my goal had been to accomplish something in my science. But then, I hit upon this stream of lava, and the heat of its fires reshaped my life. That was the primal stuff which compelled me to work upon it, and my works are a more or less successful endeavor to incorporate this incandescent matter into the contemporary picture of the world.[17]

My contention here is that The Red Book is also a record of an achievement of Jung's self-experimentation—an achievement that has largely been overlooked and which therefore constitutes what I call Jung's hidden legacy, a legacy that, as we will see, springs from the form of The Red Book, in contrast to its content.[18]

Both the Introduction and Translator's Note give mention to the form of The Red Book. Shamdasani names it as a work of psychology in a literary form and locates it in the context of the fervor of experimental activity of the early 20th century:

The first few decades of the twentieth century saw a great deal of experimentation in literature, psychology, and the visual arts. Writers tried to throw off the limitations of representational conventions to explore and depict the full range of experience—dreams, visions, and fantasies.

Many examples follow which lead to this conclusion:

We stand today on the other side of a divide between psychology and literature. To consider Liber Novus today is to take up a work that could have emerged only before these separations had been firmly established. Its study helps us understand how the divide occurred.[19]

Later on, in the Translator's Note we read:

At the outset of Liber Novus, Jung experienced a crisis of language. The spirit of the depths, who immediately challenges Jung's use of language along with the spirit of the time, informs Jung that on the terrain of his soul his achieved language will no longer serve. His own powers of knowing and speaking can no longer account for why he utters what he says or under what compulsion he speaks ... He is made to understand that what he might say on these occasions is both "madness" and, instructively, what is ...

The language in Liber Novus pursues three main stylistic registers ... One of them faithfully reports the fantasies and inner dialogues of Jung's imaginal encounters, while a second remains firmly and discerningly conceptual.

Still a third writes in a mantic and prophetic, or Romantic and dithyrambic, mode.[20]

Shamdasani's claim that the form of The Red Book marks a historical moment prior to the separation between psychology and literature opens our eyes to Jung's contribution to their subsequent separation, even while writing The Red Book. His famous and programmatic statement to Salome ("this is not art") has been thoroughly interrogated as the origin of a "doctrinal" split that subsequently opened between Jungian psychology and art.[21]

Shortly before his death in 2011, James Hillman held a series of conversations with Shamdasani regarding the perplexities of The Red Book. These conversations were subsequently published.[22] Much of the discussion focusses on the question of the form of The Red Book.[23] Both men speak of Jung's struggle to articulate a language that "evokes the poetic basis of mind" or allows the psyche to speak itself—a metaphorical language that gives voice to "the dead". Here are some excerpts from the Second and Twelfth Conversations that can give a flavor of both Hillman's and Shamdasani's search to understand the form of The Red Book:

JH: How do you find the language for what's happening?
SS: ... in a way, without realizing it, he's throwing off an outmoded conception of art ... the other movement he wishes to avoid, which is, this is revelation, simply present the material as it is ... (44-5)
If one looks at those questions in Jung's own practice, in regard to the Red Book, one sees here a situation where what

he eschews is conceptual language. At that point he realizes conceptual language is inadequate to encapsulate the language of the soul. It is the language of the soul, as far as he's concerned, because it is his dialogue to and with his soul. A new language is needed. It's a literary language but it's not a fictional language, he's quite adamant on this point. It is all Wahrheit [truth] and not Dichtung [poetry], as he says to Cary Baynes, and he struggles with this. He has to use a language that conveys, that evokes the emotional power of the experiences in question. (193)[24]

But at the end of this conversation, both men seem to remain unsettled by what exactly Jung is trying to articulate, or to give expression to. Elsewhere, Shamdasani settles on this summary of the confusion:

SS: I think there are several important things to focus on here. First, Barbara Hannah reports that Jung stated his greatest torment was a torment of not understanding. There is an overriding desire to comprehend, to understand. The second element there is within Jung's work on the images. There are two levels of comprehension. The first is within the Red Book itself, in this layer two, lyrical elaboration, and the second is within his attempt to translate this into conceptual language. Therein occurs a destruction. He's already comprehending the images in the second layer, he's already trying to look at the significance, but there is an evocation that takes place there that to my mind gets lost when he attempts to formulate it into a scientific psychology: and the word "science" is absolutely critical for him.
JH: So he can't get rid of his own first kind of thinking?
SS: No, he can't. He wrestles with the images, he wrestles with this language, which at the other side he himself is attracted to, and there's a tension.[25]

Hillman seems to believe, based on his own psychological project (Archetypal Psychology)[26], that Jung is engaging the fictional characters as a fictional character himself—a process quite familiar to writers such as Lewis Carroll whose Alice, an ordinary little girl, enters fictional reality and works within its categories of experience, as a fictional character herself. She engages the caterpillar, Mad Hatter, etc. completely on their terms, while in Wonderland.

In support of Hillman's claim, Shamdasani offers a passage from The Red Book in which a figure (the serpent soul) speaks to Jung saying, "I give you payment in images. Behold."[27] This passage is meant to support the thesis that Jung's language is the language of image, of metaphor, the language of fictional or imaginal reality. As the passage continues, Jung is presented with fictional figures such as Salome and, like Alice did in Wonderland, he takes her completely seriously, on her own (fictional) terms. A long engagement follows between Salome and Jung's "I" which would seem to be an exemplary example of what Hillman means by "evoking a poetic basis of mind".

However, if we look more closely at this text, "I give you payment in images," we can see that the structure of consciousness underlying the text (i.e., its "syntax") is not simply poetic or metaphorical or the language of image. A purely fictional figure (the serpent) is explicitly talking in terms of the concept of "images" i.e., as a consciousness that is external to image altogether, i.e., empirical consciousness.[28] The structure of consciousness involved in this text (and there are many other examples throughout the The Red Book) is that of Jung's being able to import categories of experience that belong to empirical reality into fictional reality, instead of the usual case of leaving them behind as the empirical "I" becomes a fictional "I", in the way Alice does when she descends into Wonderland. The only time Alice does employ external categories of experience from within the fictional reality that is Wonderland ("you're nothing but a pack of cards!") is also the moment that she departs fictional reality and wakes up again in empirical reality.

Amazingly, Jung was able to maintain external categories of experience while remaining "in" fictional reality. We simply have no name for this form of literature and for the kind of consciousness that gives rise to it![29]

Both Hillman and Shamdasani appear to overlook this complexity in "syntax" in their analysis of The Red Book which, once seen, reveals the reason neither commentator (Hillman or Shamdasani), nor Jung himself, can so easily settle the question of the nature of the form or "genre" that The Red Book expresses.

The Red Book is not merely a text that gives us a language expressing imaginal reality (as separate from empirical reality). To think only in these terms forces a kind of oscillation between known categories (fictional reality/empirical reality)—an oscillation that Jung presents in the different sections of The Red Book and which the translators call "polyphonic".[30] To their great credit, the translators did not try to sort out this mix of literary styles but let it remain as Jung presents it, in the spirit of letting:

Jung remain a man who was pulled loose from his moorings but also caught up in the maelstrom that has gone by the name of literary modernism. We have tried neither to modernize not to render more archaic the language and forms in which he couched his personal record.[31]

To leave Jung's text in its original polyphonic form— a mix of reporting, reflective, and mantic or dithyrambic styles is an editorial decision for which we must remain eternally grateful. In doing so the editors have prepared the possibility for future readers to perceive, with the appropriate preparation (see below), within the polyphonic language of The Red Book, a new world or reality emerging as an inception, from the "pre-world". It is this world-disclosing aspect of language that Heidegger is concerned with:

What is unspoken is not merely something that lacks voice, it is what remains unsaid, what is not yet shown, what has not yet reached its appearance. That which must remain wholly unspoken is held back in the unsaid, abides in concealment as unshowable, is mystery. That which is spoken to us speaks as dictum in the sense of something imparted, something whose speaking does not even require to be sounded. ... The essential being of language is Saying as Showing.[32]

The Red Book, I hope to show here, is a text that inaugurates an entirely new genre of literature and as such is Jung's great achievement and legacy to us. This genre expresses the inception of a new world in which our current one (empirical reality vs. fictional "unreality") is overcome (without, however, losing their distinction!). This new world appears to be one in which fictional reality (or "unreality" today) gains, by a kind of violent incursion, the same status of reality as empirical reality, within empirical reality, and it does so by penetrating into empirical reality on an equal ontological footing, as it were—a startling and perplexing state of affairs as we shall see.

The form of writing in The Red Book expresses/describes a new reality, one inaugurated by the objective psyche as its own answer to the pressing and urgent question of our times. It worked its will through the man Jung, as from the "future", and later was named by Jung as the coming guest.[33] This answer is the still implicit background of an emerging reality— a creative response by the objective psyche to the modern world condition, the truth of which Jung understood and suffered throughout his life.

It appears that, for historical reasons, Jung turned away from addressing this strange new reality theoretically, thus abandoning his achievement, in favor of his subsequent pursuit of a psychology dressed entirely in the categories of external reflection. Jung felt his "empiricism" would be acceptable to the science of the day and, at the same time, could address the world's condition. There is no question in my mind, however, that Jung experienced the new reality in its fullness and became unstable as a result. This is because, as I will show, the appearance of the new reality cannot be understood in terms of known categories of experience. In fact it destroys fundamental categories (such as inner/outer, linear temporal categories, and most importantly for my discussion, the categories of empirical/fictional). Jung therefore went through a personal experience of a "world catastrophe" (in sharp contrast to a "mere" personal breakdown, or psychosis), as former categories of experience held apart by our modern consciousness collide self-destructively on the way to forming a new reality and world.

Jung was quite aware of this aspect of "world catastrophe" during his confrontation with the unconscious. He reports two apocalyptic visions in 1913, which he first interpreted in terms of a menacing psychosis. When the world war broke out, he then interpreted the same visions empirically.[34] Jung here clearly oscillates between an inner and outer meaning as he tries unsuccessfully to account for a catastrophic breakdown in those very categories of empirical reality/fictional reality that he attempted to maintain in his interpretations.

To catch a glimpse of this breakdown and simultaneous emergence of a new world appearing from within the polyphonic presentation of The Red Book requires a kind of initiatory preparation. As I said earlier, when I turned to the newly published Liber Novus, I underwent a hermeneutic event in which the burning and pressing question of our times, already imposing itself on me for some time, became further illuminated in Jung's text. What was the nature of that preparation and how did it open my eyes to Jung's version of the question that he wrestled with throughout his life, in one way or another?

PREPARATION for a HERMENEUTIC EXPERIENCE of THE RED BOOK

Although there must be many forms of "active" imagination today, Jung's version is based firmly on his experiences as recorded in The Red Book. Yet it is easy to misunderstand his "method", so strange and disorienting it can be to ordinary consciousness, if we look carefully at his recorded experiences throughout The Red Book. Jung later makes clear what "active" means to him, during the course of an informal discussion in which he tells a story of one of his pupils who was:

> unable to conceive of the autonomy of the imagination and could not bring himself to use the method of "active imagination". Jung advised him to pay attention to his hypnagogic images. And he did so. Thus he saw a rock wall on which a goat appeared. Suddenly the animal turned its head, and the subject was seized with panic …[35]

A compelling and illuminating example of the mistake people can make in attempting to practice the kind of active imagination that Jung meant is described in another, famous book—the autobiography of Gopi Krishna who underwent an long spiritual ordeal. He suffered a spontaneous eruption of Kundalini energies that completely transformed his life:

> Long practice had accustomed me to sit in the same posture for hours at a time without the least discomfort, and I sat breathing slowly and rhythmically, my attention drawn towards the crown of my head, contemplating an imaginary lotus in full bloom, radiating light.
> I sat steadily, unmoving and erect, my thoughts uninterruptedly centered on the shining lotus, intent on keeping my attention from wandering and bringing it back again whenever it moved in any other direction.[36]

So far, many would agree that this practice is a form of "active" imagination (the lotus, or his attention, was "moving" autonomously) but when Krishna goes on, it becomes clear how different this practice is to the form of active imagination that Krishna (and Jung) discovered:

During one such spell of intense concentration I suddenly felt a strange sensation below the base of the spine, … [M]y attention was forcibly drawn towards it …[37]

After several trial and error experiments with his will (compare with Jung's willed descent)[38], Krishna reports:

Suddenly, with a roar like that of a waterfall, I felt a stream of liquid light entering my brain through the spinal cord.

Entirely unprepared for such a development, I was taken completely by surprise, … The illumination grew brighter and brighter, the roaring louder. I experienced a rocking sensation and then found myself slipping out of my body, entirely enveloped in a halo of light … I felt the point of consciousness that was myself growing wider, surrounded by waves of light. …[39]

Krishna discovered this distinction between forms of active imagination through an initiatory experience and it is the second form, whose phenomenology is so utterly different to that of the first, that gives us a clue to the nature of Jung's active imaginations in The Red Book and, as well, to his hidden legacy.

I gained access to Gopi Krishna's book and the above distinction he drew during the last decades of the 20th century when I underwent an analogous ordeal, lasting twenty years or so. This essay is not intended to be "confessional" but I will include here a detail of my ordeal that will illuminate the kind of sustained experiences that opened my eyes to Jung's text in The

Red Book and produced a hermeneutic event of understanding.[40]

One night, as I lay alone in bed (described in the third person):

At the peak of his ecstasies, he met a being that he called his Beloved Star Sister. She came to him while he was fully awake, alone in his bed. He could get out of bed and see quite clearly with his outer vision that he was alone yet he also saw, felt, and touched her there beside him, as real as his knowledge that he was alone. Both realities were interpenetrating each other. It was then that he experienced himself as being loved by another, totally as an object of divine desire. Here he learned that the human body is able to receive an influx of love from the Beyond. The heart is the door and it is the self-imposed limitations of the ego that close the door. He felt fearful that he could not contain it and was told again and again by his divine lover that he could, that he needed only to open up completely, right to the level of the cells of his body. He discovered that he could do this and that in that condition of complete surrender he received the poetry that later came to him.[41]

We can see that in both Krishna's and my account there is an "impossible" (i.e., beyond current categories of experience) yet real happening in which the ordinary domains of empirical reality and fictional (un)reality, normally held apart in modernity, unite or interpenetrate in a new way that modern consciousness with its subject-object logic cannot grasp. Krishna says, for example, that he saw a stream of liquid light (purely fictional reality) enter his brain through the spinal cord (empirical reality). With an equal force of conviction I saw a woman (fictional reality) lie down beside my body and make love to me. Yet I knew I was alone (empirical reality) as Krishna knew he was alone at the time. Through this and many other similar transforming and destabilizing experiences, I slowly came to understand that a new reality is appearing, one that requires a breakdown of our current form of consciousness and its correlative world.

Of course the fear of madness was very close throughout this period of my life and I searched far and wide for amplificatory material, such as Gopi Krishna's book, which could show me that others had undergone similar ordeals in modern life. It was during this search that I discovered some available excerpts from The Red Book, along with other examples of Jung's writing, and found what I was looking for. Later, of course, The Red Book was published and I found further confirmation of my conviction that The Red Book is a record of Jung's involvement in the same process of breakdown of categories—the psyche's response to the "pressing and urgent question of our times", a response that is hidden in the form of the complex polyphonic text—a new genre of literature that originates the appearance of a new world and a new structure of consciousness.

During the twenty years of my own ordeal, I was severely marginalized by my ever-increasingly strange experiences. Yet, at the same time, I felt an inner demand to take them seriously and to work at giving them form in the real world. I found that if I led with knowing i.e. writing down what I already knew, or leading with my thinking function, then my writing dried up, and I revealed myself to be rather a poor thinker indeed. However if I began with what emerged into consciousness, with what quickened within me, following its hints, then a very different kind of writing emerged. It lacked formal precision, or predictable prosaic structures, but it was alive!

At first this style was very disconcerting as it took me beyond the established and recognized forms of prose that would receive acceptance in journals etc. It insisted on itself, for example, during the entire duration of my Ph.D. program, which was cause for tremendous anxiety. I could not write any other way and yet what would academia think of it? I still look back on those years of toil and wonder if any other Ph.D. has been born from a literal dream. Yes, my entire program had begun with a dream and by my methodology of following the hint of the dream no matter where it led. What began with a trickle soon became a torrent. I wrote 10-12 hours a day for three years. I had to "invent" a research methodology that would support such work and, finally, it was accepted.[42]

As this process deepened, I began to trust the style of writing that I had been engaged in for many years. It was and still remains a style that I describe elsewhere as:

… a spontaneous weaving of realities that we normally keep well apart. The writing moves from a memory to a dream to a reflection of an external event, to an etymological study of a word, to the words of another author until the usual separation of inner and outer dissolves. The process involves memories of a kind of dual consciousness, interweaving of past present and future, inner and outer reality, along with philosophical thoughts expressed in direct speech, which come to the author quite spontaneously.[43]

Through these kinds of disorienting and, at times, violent encounters, I was opened up to my version of the urgent and pressing problem of our times. Many years of distillation followed and gradually the raw psychic material that had at first overwhelmed me, became the background "thinking" (i.e., effective history—Gadamer) of my consciousness, continuing to inform my perceptions, and attuning me to other appearances of this new world, a world in which fictional (un)reality and empirical reality were interpenetrating or uniting in an entirely new way, destroying at the same time their prior meaning. I was thus prepared for my encounter with The Red Book, an encounter that had the phenomenology of a hermeneutic event of understanding. I perceived the same new world appearing through the polyphonic style of the text of The Red Book.

Jung's question was and became my question.

JUNG'S HIDDEN LEGACY

In writing The Red Book, one of the intriguing aspects about Jung's methodology that commanded Hillman and Shamdasani's attention is whether he wrote while experiencing his encounters or afterwards, upon reflection. In my view this is a critical detail:

JH: I wanted to ask you about that. Does he record as it happens? Or does he record after he's had the dialogues? Because when I did active imagination myself long ago most of it was done as it happened. So it was a writing, in a way. Some of it was not. Some of it was a conversation, interior, and then I would write it—recapture it— by writing.

SS: This is one of the imponderable questions of which I've hit my head against the wall for many a year now in that it's hard to make a decision on this. Certain segments of the text give the sense that he sees a dramatic sequence and then notes it down, whereas certain other segments of the text appear to unfold in the writing.

JH: Unfold in the writing as a flowing dialogue.

SS: Yes. Or there are certain statements that I like. There's one point where he says, "I've run out of tobacco so I can't write anymore."

JH: That's good.

SS: My intuition leans to this as a writing experience, but again you can't be sure about this. Just looking at the materiality of the text suggests to me as a writer that he's writing this out.[44]

I also believe there is sufficient evidence to indicate that Jung wrote much of The Red Book while participating in the fictional realm, but as an empirical ego.[45] In other words the text of The Red Book is a record of a new form of consciousness emerging, constituting at the same time, a new world.

In the following passage, a murdered child and a woman standing by, whose face is covered by a veil, confront Jung, while within fictional reality. To his horror, the woman demands that he eat the liver of the child, but he complies:

I kneel down on the stone, cut off a piece of the liver and put it in my mouth. My gorge rises— tears burst from my eyes—cold sweat covers my brow—a dull sweet taste of blood—I swallow with desperate efforts—it is impossible— once again and once again—I almost faint—it is done. The horror has been accomplished.[46]

We are not here merely reading an imaginative account of what it would be like to eat the liver of a murdered little girl. If it were such an account, we could compare this graphic description with many other, equally compelling, and perhaps even more fascinating horror stories such as those by Edgar Allen Poe, or Dante's journey through Inferno. In other words this is not an account of a character or fictional "I" having a gruesome adventure.

We are instead witnessing a first-hand account of the actual experience of the empirical Jung while in the realm of fantasy. Jung is not in the fantasy as a fictional "I", as Dante was in The Divine Comedy, but as the empirical "I". The Red Book is analogous to reading a diary or a grotesque first-hand report of an actual act of cannibalism with the unheard-of twist that here, although Jung's reactions are empirical, the act is purely fictional! Moreover, this text suggests that, as well as Jung's "forcing his way" into fictional reality as an empirical ego, fictional reality itself was forcing itself "into" Jung. Empirical reality is here being penetrated by fictional reality, both categories breaking down in the process. It appears that the psyche is intending to produce, through new language, a literary form that expresses a process of an interpenetration or union of (what were formerly) fictional and empirical realities—a new form of consciousness that is yet to find its own language.

There is another compelling example of this process with which Jung participates:

A wreath of fire shines around the stone. I am seized with fear at what I see … I see the cross, the removal of the cross, the mourning. How agonizing the sight is! No longer do I yearn—I see the divine child, with the white serpent in his right hand, and the black serpent in his left hand. … I see the cross and Christ on it in his last hour and torment—at the foot of the cross the black serpent coils itself—it has wound itself around my feet—I am held fast and I spread my arms wide. Salome draws near. The serpent has wound itself around my whole body, and my countenance is that of a lion.[47]

There are other writers who are presenting similar mind-bending accounts of this strange new reality.[48] For example, Charles Williams fictionally explores the same phenomenon throughout his books. He narrates one such event:

She was where he had left her, but a dreadful change was coming over her. Her body was writhing into curves and knots where she lay, as if cramps convulsed her. Her mouth was open but she could not scream; her hands were clutching at her twisted throat. In her wide eyes there was now no malice, only an agony, and gradually all her body and head were drawn up backwards from the floor by an invisible force, so that from the hips she remained rigidly upright and her legs lay stretched straight out behind her on the ground, as if a serpent in human shape raised itself before him …

The face rounded out till it was perfectly smooth, with no hollows or depressions, and from her nostrils and her mouth something was thrusting out. In and out of her neck and hands another skin was forming, over or under her own—he could not distinguish which, but growing through it, here a coating, there an underveiling. Another and an inhuman tongue was flickering out over a human face …[49]

C. S. Lewis makes a very pertinent evaluation of Williams' powerful and enigmatic work, in a lecture:

[In Williams' novels]: We meet, on the one hand, very ordinary modern people who talk the slang of our own day and who live in the suburbs. On the other hand we also meet the supernatural— ghosts, magicians, and archetypal beasts. The first thing to grasp is that this not a mixture of two literary kinds. That's what some readers suspect and resent. They acknowledge on the one hand straight fiction: the classical novel, as we know it from Fielding to Goldsworthy. They acknowledge on the other the pure fantasy which creates a world of its own cut off in a kind of ringed fence, from reality—books like Wind in the Willows ... and they complain that Williams is asking them to skip to and fro from one to the other in the same work. But Williams is really writing a third kind of book which belongs to neither class and has a different value from either. He is writing that sort of book in which we begin by saying, "Let us suppose that this everyday world were at some one point invaded by the marvelous".[50]

Both Williams and Lewis seem to be intuitively pointing to the kind of reality that Jung actually gave birth to in writing The Red Book! But, importantly, where Williams was writing fictionally about this new reality, Jung was actually giving birth to it.

In my book, Manifesting Futures: Towards a New Genre of Literature, I explore further distinctions between established genres and what seems here to be Jung's "marginal practice" in Heidegger's sense, i.e., a practice that could lead to an art form that actually reconfigures and manifests our understanding of a new way of being, i.e., a new world.[51]

For example, Phillip K. Dick was a science fiction writer who underwent an ordeal lasting eight years. Dick's version of the same marginal practice that Jung inaugurated can usefully be approached by a study of his book Valis, in conjunction with his posthumously published Exegesis which is a partial collection of Dick's "mad" writings as he tried to come to grips with a revelation he had in 1974: "a sudden, discorporating slippage into vast and total knowledge that he would spend the rest of his life explicating, or exegeting."[52] [53] [54]

The posthumous publication of some of these texts highlights Dick's long and arduous attempt to understand what exactly was happening to him, in a similar manner to C. G. Jung's efforts, as recorded in The Red Book. I can choose any page at random to get a feel for sheer movement taking place, on-rushing fervor, a furor, gathering rapids, as punctuation breaks down, or ceases really to matter, as an onrushing life begins to prevail. It's like navigating a maelstrom at times, with little islands of stable meaning emerging only to be swept away again. The structure of Exegesis is described as "a freewheeling voice that ranges through personal confession, esoteric scholarship, dream accounts, and fictional figures … one of the most improbable and mind-altering manuscripts ever brought to light."[55]

This kind of writing cannot be categorized because it is expressive of a breakdown of fundamental categories such as inner/outer, linear past, present, and future, and empirical/fictional, those very categories that constitute the background of our stabilized modern structure of consciousness with its correlative empirical world.

One of the other significant category breakdowns relevant to Dick's writing is that of the pair of opposites: doing and reflection.[56] We consider these concepts a pair of opposites within our modern structure of consciousness. We can do something in life or reflect on something in life but not both at the same time.[57] In the kind of writing that Dick and Jung performed, it seems that both happen simultaneously or something else happens that subsumes both within itself. I call this "happening" participation, after Owen Barfield.[58] Dick participates with the mind in its breakdown and writes it as he participates with it, as Jung apparently did too. Thus, participation can be sharply distinguished from automatic writing where the writer's consciousness plays no part. It is also different from having an experience and subsequently writing about that experience from memory. The writing that emerges from this participatory process therefore is a form, or better, a forming (it's probably too early to call it a genre).

Such writing will appear crazy, as writers of this emerging marginal practice are forced to express mind-bending notions that are faithful to the phenomenon yet incoherent when subjected to the requirements of our stable modern form of consciousness.

A key methodological approach in producing this kind of "mad" writing is that the author takes seriously whatever phenomenon presents itself, in its own terms. The author must be able to remain "within" the phenomenon long enough so that it can teach her what it means in terms of its own logic, no matter how crazy it may sound when appraised from the categories of our current form of consciousness. The author is thus compelled to think self-presentational thoughts that defy ordinary rationality, as they think themselves out in her. For example, Dick had to learn to think the following self-presentational thought which reversed everything he knew:

The single most striking realization that Fat [Dick's alter ego—my insert] had come to was his concept of the universe as irrational and governed by an irrational mind, the creator deity. If the universe were taken to be rational, not irrational, then something breaking into it might seem irrational, since it would not belong. But Fat, having reversed everything, saw the rational breaking into the irrational. The immortal plasmate had invaded our world and the plasmate was totally rational, whereas our world is not. This structure forms the basis of Fat's world-view. It is the bottom line.[59]

Valis and Exegesis are both accounts of the real process that a human being undergoes if she is pulled into participation with the mind as it undergoes an epochal breakdown, so that all the categories that support modern consciousness (especially spatial and temporal categories) go under, taking the author with them, sometimes into insanity, but as we can see with Phillip K. Dick, also into sanity, the kind of sanity that our normal consciousness will judge as insane.

In just one small example that suggests strongly an incursion of fictional reality into empirical reality, Dick recounts, during a speech:

The subject of this speech is a topic which has been discovered recently and which may not exist at all … It's a common theme in my writing that a dark-haired girl shows up at the door of the protagonist and tells him that his world is delusional, there is something false about it. Well, this did finally happen to me. I even knew that her hair would be black. I had an actual complete sense of what she would look like and what she would say. She did appear. She was a total stranger and she did inform me of this fact: some of my fictional works were, *in a literal sense* [my emphasis], true.[60]

This art form cannot only be deliberate, even though I said earlier that Jung willed his way into fictional reality. Giegerich convincingly shows that as a whole, the experience of The Red Book "was a deliberate technical undertaking", although "[t]here was certainly spontaneity within this experiment and for the experiencing subject."[61]

The Red Book does not simply represent an *avant-garde* art movement with its conscious program. Throughout Jung's accounts of his psychic experiences, as recorded in The Red Book, as well as his autobiography and other publications, he insists that the encounters he has with imaginal figures are "spontaneous", "immediate", "autonomous", with a "compelling presence", "unintentional" etc.

In a similar way, Philip K. Dick engaged in deliberate experimentation (such as massive doses of vitamins, or amphetamines) during his eight-year long ordeal, within which, like Jung, he experienced many spontaneous happenings that convinced him of alternate realities as well.

This complex phenomenology points to an unheard-of "art form" in the making, one that "requires" a union/breakdown of differences: empirical reality with its correlative (willful, unitary) consciousness and fictional reality with its will as displayed in a plurality of consciousnesses:

Supposing that nothing else is "given" as real but our world of desires and passions, that we cannot sink or rise to any other "reality" but just that of our impulses—for thinking is only a relation of these impulses to one another:—are we not permitted to make the attempt and to ask the question whether this which is "given" does not SUFFICE, by means of our counterparts, for the understanding even of the so-called mechanical (or "material") world? ... Granted, finally, that we succeeded in explaining our entire instinctive life as the development and ramification of one fundamental form of will—namely, the Will to Power, as my thesis puts it ... one would thus have acquired the right to define ALL active force unequivocally as WILL TO POWER. The world seen from within, the world defined and designated according to its "intelligible character"—it would simply be "Will to Power," and nothing else.[62]

Apparently, for fictional reality to make an impression on such a modern consciousness that Nietzsche describes here, it must appear as a stronger will, one that subjects the willful modern ego to its experiments. Only then can fictional reality initiate the modern ego into its, fictional reality's, reality, i.e., having the same ontological status as empirical reality, but remaining as "fictional" within "empirical" reality— a new reality altogether!

As The Red Book testifies, Jung strove mightily to understand what was happening to him. Nowhere have I found a more compelling effort to understand than in his description of "suspension" as it appears in the seminars on Nietzsche's Thus Spake Zarathustra.[63] This appears to be shortly after he emerged from his "confrontation with the unconscious". With a little more distance from his wrenching experiences, he now seemed able to further the task of understanding his ordeal. In the seminars, Jung turns to the motif of suspension that appears in Nietzsche's book at the point where Zarathustra "buries the corpse in a hollow tree."[64] In one of Jung's inspired moments, he amplifies quickly around the image of the corpse in the tree until he settles on the motif of suspension from which an explosion of amplificatory images emerges (see below).

Jung's interpretation of this motif clearly is also a disclosure of (what became) the "effective history" of his own ordeal, now informing his hermeneutic exposition of Nietzsche's work. Yet it is so difficult to understand that, to date, no one has subsequently explored or developed this notion of suspension any further, in terms of the material of The Red Book, as far as I know.[65]

Perhaps the most significant reason that Jung's discussion of suspension is so difficult to grasp is that it is impossible to language in terms of current categories of thought. Jung's years-long ordeal, as recorded in The Red Book was a sustained experience of suspension as he encountered purely fictional figures empirically. If the images of fictional reality are first and foremost figures of speech, then we are approaching a profound mystery of language when we undergo such experiences with them, as Jung did:

For the great mystery … is this: the appearance of a speaking figure, the very embodiment as it were in human-divine form of clear, articulated, play-related and therefore enchanting, language—its appearance in that deep primordial darkness where one expects only animal muteness, wordless silence, or cries of pleasure and pain.[66]

In my view Jung's ordeal was first and foremost an undergoing of such an experience with language, also in the sense that Heidegger means:

To undergo an experience with something [here language— my insert] means that this something, which we reach along the way in order to attain it, itself pertains to us, meets and makes its appeal to us, in that it transforms us into itself …

We speak and speak about language. What we speak of, language, is always ahead of us. Our speaking merely follows language constantly. Thus we are continually lagging behind … Accordingly, when we speak of language we remain entangled in a speaking that is persistently inadequate.[67]

Thus, when Jung attempts to interpret the motif of suspension as he saw it appearing in Thus Spake Zarathustra, springing as he did from the soil of his own suspension, he is forced to draw amplificatory material from the wide resource of his own scholarly background. For example he speaks of suspension as (with some paraphrasing):

an aspect of crucifixion;
the unconscious aspect of transfiguration;

transformation [as being] the fate of the body;

transfiguration [as being] the fate of the subtle body;

preceding birth or creation;

incubation of the subtle body;

producing superior knowledge [like Odin's suspension and the art of writing];

identification of the creator with what he is going to bring forth;

torment in order to embody or incarnate the unconscious contents;

giving body to the suspended potentialities of the unconscious;

giving body to one's thoughts through "artistic" production;

ideas that express themselves as bodily symptoms;

unconscious contents that "eat the sacrificed body" so that they can incarnate;

ideas that take possession of the body;

an initiatory process of "denying the body", inflicting terrible suffering so that a body can be produced in the mind.[68]

In reading the transcript of Jung's seminars, including the section on the motif of suspension, I am struck by the sheer force and flow of his extemporaneous language which seems to be a fountain or spring, flowing over with images drawn from scholarship but, at the same time, revivified by new meaning, as Jung appropriates (in the sense of hermeneutics) Nietzsche's work to his efforts of giving voice to his own violent ordeal of suspension during the production of The Red Book.

For all Jung's efforts in the Seminar and subsequently throughout his life, this process of suspension remains a profound mystery and has received little attention by subsequent commentators.

For example, as I said earlier, Hillman at times seems to take another view. He believes that Jung's work validates:

> ... what I felt I was doing all these years without knowing it. I mean, my therapy of myself and my therapy with others, whenever possible, focused on active imagination, dialogues, encounters with figures, and teaching and learning how to deal with figures. So personification seemed to me absolutely the essential activity of the psyche, just as Jung says, or shows, in the Red Book. [69]

This interpretation of The Red Book simply assimilates Jung's work to Hillman's project (Archetypal Psychology) and largely ignores the phenomenology of the ordeal, which involves the empirical Jung as he encountered fictional reality, in a condition of suspension. One can, after all, learn the practice of "seeing through" to the archetypal background of modern phenomena, without in the least becoming "suspended".

Wolfgang Giegerich certainly acknowledges the phenomenon of torture in The Red Book and goes to considerable lengths in analyzing it as a soul phenomenon.[70] [71] His project is to show how Jung's notion of the unconscious, as a positivized factual reality within the empirical man, was "installed" in the first place:

> A prolonged step-by-step process of sinking the form of thought into the form of the individual's ... existential experience "in the flesh."
>
> This is a process which to a large extent has the nature of a painful suffering (up to the point of near-madness) and

is accordingly experienced as "cruel," a very frequent word in The Red Book. The torment was absolutely necessary to really, and absolutely convincingly, install the new arena in factual, bodily felt existence, in man as mere Dasein.[72]

There can be no doubt that, as Giegerich claims, Jung later codified some of the phenomena of his ordeal into a dogma concerning the nature of god and his psychology of the unconscious:

I cannot conceive of any religious belief that is less than a violation of my ego-consciousness;
[Individuation] involves suffering, a passion of the ego: the ordinary empirical man ... suffers, so to speak, from the violence done to him from the Self;
God is an apt name given to all overpowering emotions in my own psychic system, subduing my conscious will and usurping control over myself;
This is the name by which I designate all things which cross my wilful path violently and recklessly, all things which upset my subjective views, plans, and intentions and change the course of my life for better or worse.[73 74 75]

But Jung's, and indeed Giegerich's interpretations, cannot exhaust the meaning of "suspension", as we will see. Giegerich's project is to valorize the unity of thinking and thought, fiction and truth. He believes that Jung tears fantasy (the form of fantasy) and truth apart as two opposite realities because (he claims) Jung wants to identify truth with factual existence, as if it [truth] were a piece of nature: "An elephant is true because it exists".[76 77]

Giegerich's analysis of the ontological "purpose" of Jung's ordeal is consistent with his (Giegerich's) view of art which he explicates by reference to Dante's Divine Comedy:

The fantasy content [of the Comedy—my insert] was relentlessly let go of and in this way allowed to find its own center of gravity and source of authority solely within itself as imaginal or fantastic …

Art-making requires taking a plunge. The fantasy (the idea, the image) is precisely allowed to be "nothing but" fantasy … And only through this going under of the artist's subjectivity into the fantasy as self-sufficient and an end in itself does the art-work also obtain true objectivity …

Art-making is the relentless working off of the duality of subject (author) versus object, experience (content) versus representation (form), origin or cause versus result, in favor of the singularity of the work of art that has everything it needs within itself. Dante's work speaks for itself … [I]t is not a report about inner experiences from "the unconscious," not his "individuation process." …[78]

It's critical for my discussion at this point to understand that Giegerich is basing his analysis of The Red Book, and his interpretation of what Jung was doing on this, his own view of what constitutes art! Thus his analysis is a vehicle for appropriating (hermeneutically) the text of The Red Book to his own project, just as Hillman did. Giegerich wants to establish psychology as the true discipline of interiority and to do so he has spent a lifetime re-working (deepening) Jung's essential psychological concepts into a more adequate form that resolves the neurotic structure of psychology that Jung constructed out of his (Jung's) subsequent interpretations of his ordeal.[79]

To establish his own psychology out of Jung's experiences, however, Giegerich relies on a conception of art and art-making that is informed by the past and by the dominant mode of being that has been hardening over centuries, as mirrored in the distinction and then disjunction between (what has now become) empirical reality or Heidegger's Dasein and fictional reality (the unreal). There can, however, be no doubt today that art forms no longer carry the same ontological weight as empirical reality, no matter how much we may be privately gripped by the truth of the Comedy etc., as Giegerich clearly is.

In fact, Hillman and Shamdasani demonstrate that Jung was caught between two notions of art, one that he may share with Giegerich and one that is still forming, still in the future. For example, they address Jung's well-known refusal in which he declares to Salome that what he is doing is not art:

SS: ... let's stick to this question of art for the moment. Jung himself maintains the nineteenth-century conception of art, so paradoxically when he says "This is not art" it is bringing him into the most radical proximity to the European avant-garde who are in the process of dismantling traditional conceptions of art. So in a way, without realizing it, he's throwing off an outmoded conception of art.
JH: That's interesting. He's throwing away, or out, an outmoded conception of art. So this is not art, meaning this is not that kind of art.[80]

This view, that Jung is struggling to articulate a new definition of art, is further supported in the work of Russell Lockhart who has devoted his life to extending

Jungian thought into the domain of art, where he believes it properly belongs. For example, he compares Jung's welcoming attitude towards art near the end of his life, as captured enigmatically in his relief sculpture on the wall at Bollingen, to his rejection, as a young man, of the speech of the anima who, in response to his question, "what am I doing," said, "it is art".[81] Lockhart goes on to quote Rosenburg's definition of the new art form:

[A]rt consists of one-person creeds, one-psyche cultures. Its direction is toward a society in which the experiences of each will be the ground of a unique, inimitable form—in short, a society in which everyone will be an artist. Art in our time can have no other social aim—an aim dreamed of by modern poets, from Lautréamont to Whitman, Joyce and the Surrealists, and in which is embodied the essence of the continuing revolt against domination by tradition.[82]

The violence, torment, and suspension that Jung experienced is necessary to the birth of this new art form. Empirical reality's status as having sole claim on reality is challenged by the unreal: fictional reality. Empirical reality insists on its supremacy and this obdurateness can only be challenged (or threatened) by another reality that can meet it on its own terms. Jung was faced with a reality that was every bit as real as empirical reality—as convincing as Johnson's rock, while at the same time, irreducible to empirical reality. Fictional reality penetrates empirical reality in a contest of wills. It is the isolated personhood of the empiricist that is violated. The penetration involves the empirically real body in a way that is yet to be languaged adequately. As I said, Jung drew from a vast reservoir of amplificatory material to try to interpret his experience of suspension. And as Wolfgang Giegerich has shown, he also produced a psychology based in part on his confused or prejudiced conceptions of what had happened to him. Giegerich has subsequently single-handedly developed an internally consistent theory and practice of depth psychology (psychology as the discipline of interiority) from within the great and confused theoretical work of the thinker Jung,[83] but what remains is to find adequate language that can give further form to the new art and the new "artist", as inaugurated by Jung in The Red Book.

It is clear to me that this language must arise from within such polyphonic accounts as The Red Book.

CONCLUSION

Although Jung participated fully in the ordinary activities that are to be found in the world today (i.e., political, economic, scientific, professional, familial, international, etc.), none of these modes of being were the focus of his concern when he said, "The great problem of our time is that we don't understand what is happening to the world."[84] The focus of this momentous statement is not the surface, external, or "positive-factual" world of Dasein but the ground or psychic background of the world of perception and experience. A shift or a transformation had occurred in this background around the early 19th century and Jung underwent an initiation that brought the truth of this transformation home to him, when he was only twelve years old.[85]

Prior to the 19th century the perceived and experienced world of human beings was (or could become) symbolic or imaginal. The world of things was still grounded in the infinite depths of the psyche, and at any time that depth could reveal itself to us, as reflected in the things of the world. Thus the things could, at times, still "speak" to us. Around the time of the Industrial Revolution, this ground disappeared completely, leaving us in a perceived world of surface only, with no depth (i.e., intelligence, wisdom, infinity, subjectivity, etc.) at all.[86] This was also the time in which personhood was invented—Heidegger's world of Dasein. It was and remains a world of "poverty of symbols", where the previous symbol-bearing things of the world (Heidegger's "things") have become mere resources.[87]

Because Jung understood this loss so fully, having been initiated into its truth, he suffered greatly throughout his life and, because he was a healer, he bent to the task of dealing with this entirely new world constitution and the suffering it brought to human beings. His psychology, the genesis of which lies in his extraordinary ordeal of suspension, as recorded in The Red Book, is a cultural form that intends to address our state of "poverty of symbols", and indeed one can argue the success of that project.[88]

The Red Book is however also an account of a momentous achievement by Jung—an achievement that I have called his hidden legacy. During the course of his ordeal, Jung found his way to the mode of being that Heidegger calls a clearing, where a new world can appear, as languaged in the polyphonic form that the editors of The Red Book rendered so faithfully for us.[89]

This clearing is also a new definition of the human being, one which can "welcome the coming guest", with a new soul capacity to be the new language—language which, to our present form of consciousness, appears "life- threatening," mad, and abyssal—the end of the world!

As the scientific world became increasingly reified, empirical reality became more privileged as the reality, while the meaning-endowing psyche increasingly became denigrated to the status of fiction (unreality). Thus our world, the condition of which Jung felt nobody understood, has appeared more and more meaningless. Jung's achievement, his hidden legacy, lies in his capacity to undergo the necessary breakdown of categories through a process that he later called suspension, towards becoming a new kind of human being in his essence, one which can embody and articulate the next historical transformation in the background of our world: from a total separation between psyche and empirical world to a newly configured background in which psychic and empirical realities are subsumed, without obliterating their difference—a new as yet unnamed reality that his polyphonic language gives first appearance to.

It appears that the psyche, that world background bearer of meaning, wishes to know itself as psyche or spirit, not separate from empirical reality (this self-knowledge being already achieved in the metaphysical world) but as the within-ness or interiority of empirical reality. This new status of reality must have its own (apocalyptic) language, of course, in order to appear in the first place and The Red Book shows us something of the nature of that language.

Russell Lockhart is also clearly aware of this emerging transformation in consciousness-world constitution. Here he is first talking about the language that supports our current empirical reality (positivism):

At the root of this is what I call the seduction of nouns and adjectives leading into a separatist language, a language in the service of rationality and linearity, insisting on subject-object distinctions. Its aim is distance, its style is prose, its claim is science, its anima is progress: getting somewhere. The language of such separation is made in sentences. But what do sentences sentence us to? Something is imprisoned in the sentence, and it yearns to be free. That freedom is found sometimes in poetry, where verse is free, where the sentence has lost its power, its throne. Poetry's language is verbs, vital and vivid verbs forcing involvement, inviting relationship rather than separation, immersion rather than distance.[90]

Lockhart goes on to give us a hint of the language that would support (in the sense of "allow to appear") a new reality that he calls "between living and dreaming", which I interpret as the clearing in which psyche and world interpenetrate in a hitherto unknown way:

How I would love to speak as psyche speaks! Then I wouldn't be chained to talking about it. But what would that be? Two compelling fantasies have hounded me. The first was literally to let the psyche speak: dreams, visions, wild synchronicities, and psychopathologies of everyday life—mine and others all mixed together without commentary, interpretation, analysis, and endless babble about meaning. A genuine theatre of the soul! Can you imagine what madness that would be? The second fantasy was to be completely silent. Imagine: complete silence, to listen to what the spontaneous psyche would say when no one was going on and on about psyche's speech.[91]

Lockhart is here, in 1982, speaking as an augur in response to Jung's auguring when he carved the enigmatic relief into the wall at Bollingen (circa 1960). Both were auguring a transformation in the psychic background of the world, the soul's own response to the pressing and urgent question of our times—a response heard, suffered, endured, and recorded by C. G. Jung in The Red Book.

END NOTES

1 Gadamer, Hans. G.: Philosophical Hermeneutics. Ed. Linge E. David. Trans. Linge E. David. University of California Press, Berkeley, 1977, 13.

2 Ibid, 12.

3 Gadamer, H. G.: Truth and Method. Trans. J. Weinsheimer & D. G. Marshall. Bloomsbury Publishing, London, 2013, 478.

4 De Beistegui, M.: The New Heidegger. Continuum Books, New York, 2005, 191–92.

5 Later reprinted in Giegerich, W.: The Flight into the Unconscious: An Analysis of C. G. Jung's Psychology Project. Spring Journal Publications, New Orleans, 2013.

6 Ibid, 1.

7 Ibid, 2.

8 Ibid.

9 Ibid, 8.

10 Ibid, 11-12.

11 Ibid, 16.

12 Ibid, 18.

13 Hugo Ball: cited and quoted in Jung, C. G.: The Red Book. Ed. S. Shamdasani. W. W. Norton & Company, New York, 2009, 194.

14 Giegerich, W.: "Psychology as Anti-Philosophy: C. G. Jung." Spring 77Philosophy & Psychology, (2007): 11-51, 18-20. By "paradise of childhood" or "God's world", Giegerich is referring to "the whole heritage of the metaphysical and mythological traditions" which ends as the new world after the Industrial Revolution emerges.

15 Jung, C. G.: The Red Book. Ed. S. Shamdasani. W. W. Norton & Company, New York, 2009, 194.

16 Owens, Lance S.: "Jung and Aion: Time, Vision, and a Wayfaring Man." Psychological Perspectives 54.3 (2011): 253-289, 257. The full quote is: "[Liber Novus] is the bedrock and foundation upon which any understanding of the life and work of C. G. Jung must be built."

17 Jung, C. G.: Memories, Dreams, Reflections. Ed. A. Jaffe. Trans. C. Winston & R. Winston. Random House, New York, 1963, 199.

18 The contents of The Red Book are largely understood, in accord with Jung's own assessment, as the "primal stuff" or basis of Jung's later psychology project, this being his putative answer to "the pressing and urgent question of our times". However, the form of the book has received much less attention, by Jung and later scholarship, in terms of how it (the form) could also constitute another, unsuspected and startling, answer to that same question.

19 Jung, C. G.: The Red Book. Ed. S. Shamdasani. W. W. Norton & Company, New York, 2009, 194.

20 Ibid, 222.

21 Hillman, James.: The Thought of the Heart. Spring Publications, Dallas, 1981, 33ff; Lockhart, Russell, A.: Psyche Speaks: A Jungian Approach to Self and the World. Chiron Publications, Wilmette, 1982, 66ff; Woodcock, John C.: Making New Worlds: The Way of the Artist. iUniverse, Bloomington, 2013; Woodcock, John C.: Animal Soul. iUniverse, Bloomington, 2012; Hillman, James & Shamdasani, Sonu.: Lament of the Dead: Psychology after Jung's Red Book. W. W. Norton & Co., London, 2013, 44ff; Giegerich, W.: "Liber Novis, that is, The New Bible. A First Analysis of C. G. Jung's Red Book." Spring 83 Minding the Animal Psyche (2010): 361-412, 364ff.

22 Hillman, James & Shamdasani, Sonu.: Lament of the Dead: Psychology after Jung's Red Book. W. W. Norton & Co., London, 2013.

23 Ibid. See in particular First and Second Conversation.

24 Hillman, James & Shamdasani, Sonu.: Lament of the Dead: Psychology after Jung's Red Book. W. W. Norton & Co., London, 2013, 44, 45, 193.

25 Ibid, 52.

26 For example, Hillman says:

"The book somehow validated what I felt I was doing all these years without knowing it. I mean, my therapy of myself and my therapy with others, whenever possible, focused on active imagination, dialogues, encounters with figures, and teaching and learning how to deal with figures. So personification seemed to me absolutely the essential activity of the psyche, just as Jung says, or shows, in the Red Book." Ibid, 79-80.

27 Jung, C. G.: The Red Book. Ed. S. Shamdasani. W. W. Norton & Company, New York, 2009, 323. Giegerich shows how such a statement as "I give you payment in images", reflects a far more complex structure of consciousness than either Hillman or Shamdasani seem to appreciate or know about. He analyses structurally equivalent statements in The Red Book, where Jung is addressing imaginal figures while, in the same breath (i.e., while remaining in fictional reality) denying their imaginal character: "See Giegerich, W.: "Liber Novis, that is, The New Bible. A First Analysis of C. G. Jung's Red Book." Spring 83 Minding the Animal Psyche (2010): 361-412, 401ff.

28 Only a structure of consciousness that is already external to psyche can speak in terms of symbols, images, metaphors, the unconscious, or indeed the psyche, as such. An image cannot talk about itself, or other imaginal figures, as an image or symbol without destroying its character as image.

29 Wolfgang Giegerich gives a penetrating analysis of these complex and overlooked structures of consciousness involved in The Red Book: Giegerich, W.: "Liber Novis, that is, The New Bible. A First Analysis of C. G. Jung's Red Book." Spring 83 Minding the Animal Psyche (2010): 361-412.

30 Jung, C. G.: The Red Book. Ed. S. Shamdasani. W. W. Norton & Company, New York, 2009, 222.

31 Ibid.

32 Heidegger, M.: On the Way to Language. Trans. P. D. Hertz. Harper, San Francisco, 1982, 122-3.

33 Jung, C. G.: C. G. Jung Letters. Ed. G. A. Adler. Trans. R. F. Hull. Vols. 2 (1951-1960). Routledge &Kegan Paul, London, 1975, 591. "We have simply got to listen to what the psyche spontaneously says to us ... It is the great dream which has spoken through the artist as mouthpiece. All his love and passion (his "values") flow towards the coming guest to proclaim his arrival ... What is the great Dream? ... It is the future and the picture of the new world, which we do not understand yet."

34 Jung, C. G.: Memories, Dreams, Reflections. Ed. A. Jaffe. Trans. C. Winston & R. Winston. Random House, New York, 1963, 175-6.

35 This story is recounted by Charles Baudouin in McGuire, William & Hull, R. F. C., ed.: C. G. Jung Speaking: Interviews and Encounters. Princeton University Press, Princeton, 1977, 236.

36 Krishna, Gopi. Living with Kundalini: The Autobiography of Gopi Krishna. Shambala, Boston, 1993, 1.

37 Ibid, 1-2

38 In Krishna's report, "my attention was forcibly drawn towards it," we see a curious mixture of "willed surrender", the same phenomenon that Jung reports: "From the beginning I had conceived my voluntary confrontation with the unconscious as a scientific experiment which I myself was conducting ... Today I might equally well say that it was an experiment which was being conducted on me." Jung, C. G.: Memories, Dreams, Reflections. Ed. A. Jaffe. Trans. C. Winston & R. Winston. Random House, New York, 1963, 178.

39 Krishna, Gopi. Living with Kundalini: The Autobiography of Gopi Krishna. Shambala, Boston, 1993, 2-3

40 Woodcock, John C.: The Imperative. iUniverse, Bloomington, 2011.

41 Ibid, 24. I wrote my autobiography as a story of "David" in order to gain some distance from the still incandescent material.

42 A record of my process through those years can be found in my book, Woodcock, John C.: Living in Uncertainty Living with Spirit. iUniverse, Bloomington, 2012, an early attempt to comprehend what I had gone through.

43 Woodcock, John C.: Animal Soul. iUniverse, Bloomington, 2012, 77.

44 Hillman, James & Shamdasani, Sonu.: Lament of the Dead: Psychology after Jung's Red Book. W. W. Norton & Co., London, 2013, 5.

45 For example, in Memories, Dreams, Reflections, 178, Jung says, "Sometimes it was as if I were hearing it with my ears, sometimes, feeling it with my mouth, as if my tongue were formulating words; now and then I heard myself whispering aloud"; also, the use of present tense, along with the immense difficulty in finding language in which the new reality can appear. The fact is this new reality cannot appear as such to current consciousness since the structure of modern consciousness (subject-object) destroys such appearance. The language of simple description, however, is just fine to a consciousness that is no longer bound by the opposites (empirical realty vs fictional reality, for example).

46 Jung, C. G.: The Red Book. Ed. S. Shamdasani. W. W. Norton & Company, New York, 2009, 290.

47 Ibid, 252.

48 I explore such forms of literature in my books. See, for example Woodcock, John C.: Manifesting Possible Futures: Towards a New Genre of Literature. iUniverse, Bloomington, 2013.

49 Williams, Charles.: The Place of the Lion. Regent College Publishing, Vancouver, 170.

50 Lewis, C. S.: C. S. Lewis Lectures on the Novels of Charles Williams. Retrieved from YouTube: https://www.youtube.com/watch?v=Z5w134gYz04, (2012, 11 29).

51 See: Dreyfus, Hubert, L.: "Heidegger's Ontology of Art", A Companion to Heidegger. Eds. H. L. Dreyfus & Mark A. Wrathall. Blackwell Publishing, Malden, 2005, 407.

52 Dick, Philip K.: Valis(S.F. Masterworks). The Orion Publishing Group, London, 1981.

53 Dick, Philip K.: The Exegesis of Philip K. Dick. Ed. P. Jackson & J. Lethem. Houghton Mifflin Harcourt, New York, 2011.

54 Ibid. From the Introduction, xiv.

55 Ibid. From the Cover (Inside Flap).

56 This is another formulation of Hillman's and Shamdasani's question whether Jung wrote during the active imagination or following it.

57 For a delightful and penetrating discussion of a variation of these opposites (expressed as enjoyment/contemplation), see Lewis, C. S.: Surprised by Joy: The Shape of My Early Life. Fount Paperbacks, Glasgow, 1980, 174.

58 Barfield, O.: Saving the Appearances: A Study in Idolatry. Faber & Faber, London, 1957.

59 Dick, Philip K.: Valis(S.F. Masterworks). Orion, London, 2010. Kindle Edition, 112.

60 Dick, Philip K. The Android Prophet. YouTube. Retrieved from http://www.youtube.com/watch?v=84csPWKNHUU.

61 Giegerich, W.: "Liber Novis, that is, The New Bible. A First Analysis of C. G. Jung's Red Book." Spring 83 Minding the Animal Psyche (2010): 361-412, 372ff.

62 Nietzsche, F.: "Beyond Good and Evil", The Complete Works of Friedrich Nietzsche (1909-1913). Trans. H. Zimmern. Project Gutenberg, www.gutenberg.org. Chapter II. The Free Spirit, par 36.

63 Jung, C. G.: Nietzsche's Zarathustra: Notes of the Seminar Given in 1934-1939. Trans. J. L. Jarrett. Princeton University Press, Princeton, 1988. As far as I know, the motif of suspension that appears in the Seminars has not yet been related to Jung's own experiences in The Red Book.

64 Ibid, 173-198. Jung first uses the term "suspension" on 187.

65 With the exception of Wolfgang Giegerich who gives a good deal of attention to the phenomenon of "torture" that occurs throughout The Red Book.

66 Kerenyi, K.: Hermes: Guide of Souls. Spring Journal Books, Dallas, 1990, 88.

67 Heidegger, M.: On the Way to Language. Trans. P. D. Hertz. Harper, San Francisco, 1982, 73-75.

68 Jung, C. G.: Nietzsche's Zarathustra: Notes of the Seminar Given in 1934-1939. Trans. J. L. Jarrett. Princeton University Press, Princeton, 1988, 187-197.

69 Hillman, James & Shamdasani, Sonu.: Lament of the Dead: Psychology after Jung's Red Book. W. W. Norton & Co., London, 2013, 79.

70 Giegerich, W.: "Liber Novis, that is, The New Bible. A First Analysis of C. G. Jung's Red Book." Spring 83 Minding the Animal Psyche (2010): 361-412, 371, 391-2.

71 Giegerich, W.: The Flight into the Unconscious: An Analysis of C. G. Jung's Psychology Project. Spring Journal Publications, New Orleans, 2013, 236ff.

72 Giegerich, W.: "Liber Novis, that is, The New Bible. A First Analysis of C. G. Jung's Red Book." Spring 83 Minding the Animal Psyche (2010): 361-412, 391ff.

73 Jung, C. G.: C. G. Jung Letters. Ed. G. A. Adler. Trans. R. F. Hull. Vols. 2 (1951-1960). Routledge &Kegan Paul, London, 1975. 2 vols, 51.

74 Jung, C. G. The Collected Works of C. G. Jung. Trans. R. F. C. Hull. Vol. 11. Princeton University Press, Princeton, 1977, Par. 233.

75 Jung, C. G.: C. G. Jung Letters. Ed. G. A. Adler. Trans. R. F. Hull. Vols. 2 (1951-1960). Routledge &Kegan Paul, London, 1975. 2 vols, 525. These quotes are cited in Giegerich, W.: The Flight into the Unconscious: An Analysis of C. G. Jung's Psychology Project. Spring Journal Publications, New Orleans, 2013, 236.

76 Giegerich, W.: "Liber Novis, that is, The New Bible. A First Analysis of C. G. Jung's Red Book." Spring 83 Minding the Animal Psyche (2010): 361-412, 366ff.

77 Interestingly, Philip K. Dick also "tears fantasy and truth apart" in a move that violates Giegerich's conception of art. Dick writes: "I am a fictionalizing philosopher, not a novelist; my novel & story- writing ability is employed as a means to formulate my perception. The core of my writing is not art but truth." Found in: Sutin, Lawrence.: Divine Invasions: A Life of Philip K. Dick. Carroll & Graf, New York, 2005. Kindle Edition, Kindle Locations 158-159. I said that Giegerich is basing his criticism of this "violation" on his well-established conception of art (he cites Dante's Divine Comedy as a counter example). But I believe that these moves by Jung and Dick are also hints towards a new definition of art, one based on the interpenetration of fictional reality with empirical reality, with which both men were intimately involved their entire lives. To achieve this, they have to negate or downgrade all previous definitions of art (as now having nothing to do with truth).

78 Giegerich, W.: "Liber Novis, that is, The New Bible. A First Analysis of C. G. Jung's Red Book." Spring 83 Minding the Animal Psyche (2010): 361-412, 365-6.

79 Giegerich, W.: The Neurosis of Psychology. Spring Journal Publications, New Orleans, 2005.

80 Hillman, James & Shamdasani, Sonu.: Lament of the Dead: Psychology after Jung's Red Book. W. W. Norton & Co., London, 2013, Second Conversation, 44.

81 Lockhart, Russell A.: Psyche Speaks: A Jungian Approach to Self and World. Chiron, Wilmette,1987, 73ff. Lockhart regards this little understood and barely mentioned high relief sculpture as an augury and shows how Jung is auguring a time of the artist soul which will welcome the coming guest. The sculpture is mentioned briefly in Jaffe, A., ed.: C. G. Jung: Word and Image. Princeton University Press, Princeton, 1979 and in a letter to Dr Tauber in Jung, C. G.: C. G. Jung Letters. Ed. G. A. Adler. Trans. R. F. Hull. Vol. 2 (1951-1960). Routledge & Kegan Paul, London, 1975. 2 vols, 615.

82 Harold Rosenburg as quoted in: Lockhart, Russell A.: Psyche Speaks: A Jungian Approach to Self and World. Chiron, Wilmette,1987, 79.

83 See http://www.ispdi.org for the International Society for Psychology as the Discipline of Interiority.

84 Heidegger speaks of worlds, or modes of being, in his existential phenomenology but none of them involve a conscious subject. See Dreyfus, H. L.: Being-in-the-World: A Commentary of Heidegger's Being and Time, Division 1. The MIT Press, Cambridge, 1995, 13.

85 Giegerich, W.: "Psychology as Anti-Philosophy: C. G. Jung." Spring 77Philosophy & Psychology, (2007): 11-52 for a full discussion of Jung's initiation into the truth of our times.

86 Giegerich, W.: Technology and the Soul. Spring Journal Publications, New Orleans, 2007, 31-34, for an excellent description of this momentous soul event. Also, Owen Barfield notes that this soul event brought forward our first attempt to understand our origins historically, in the form of Darwinian evolution, an evolution of idols, as Barfield says. See Barfield, O.: Saving the Appearances: A Study in Idolatry. Faber & Faber, London, 1957, n. 55. Although historical research has long pointed to the Industrial Revolution in the 19th century as a turning point in history, the same research has understood this

change in terms of the dominant fantasy of progress, as advanced by prominent individuals. Michel Foucault's "archeology of thought" is a contrasting historical method that allows the "rejected and marginalized" also to speak and has therefore yielded very different results. He also points to the great discontinuity occurring in the early 19th century but understands it as a transformation in our "mode of being": "[I]t was simply that the mode of being of things, and of the order that divided them up before presenting them to the understanding, was profoundly altered." Language ceases to be representative of the things and becomes instead "historical" in its mode of being. Things lose their imaginal depths and become positivized (e.g., hidden organic structure). See Foucault, M.: The Order of Things: An Archeology of the Human Sciences. Random House, New York, 1994, Preface.

87 See Der Spiegel, "Interview with Martin Heidegger", 1966, for Heidegger's understanding of technology and the ontological status of "things" today.

88 Giegerich, W.: "Liber Novis, that is, The New Bible. A First Analysis of C. G. Jung's Red Book." Spring 83 Minding the Animal Psyche (2010): 361-412 for a deep analysis of The Red Book as a record of the actual process of installation of the Jungian unconscious.

89 "Heidegger takes note of Heraclitus's use of the image of lightning to describe the context created by the way being unifies what-is: Heraclitus says both that logos steers all things through all things and that the thunderbolt steers all things. Heidegger's own notion of this cultural context as a "lightening" or "clearing" in which things show themselves plays on this same imagery. The logos lets everything be gathered into a unified totality, but our understanding of the character of this totality can be changed in a flash - a lightning flash of insight which casts new illumination on our world." See White, Carol:

"Heidegger and the Greeks". A Companion to Heidegger. Ed. H. L. Dreyfus & M. A. Wrathall. Blackwell Publishing, Malden, Kindle Edition, 2005, location 2447.

90 Lockhart, Russell A.: Psyche Speaks: A Jungian Approach to Self and World. Chiron, Wilmette,1987, 85. Lockhart is a Jungian Analyst who gave the inaugural lectures for the C. G. Jung Foundation for Analytical Psychology, in 1982. The aim of these lecture series was to make an original contribution to Jungian thought.

91 Ibid. 7. Linda Hutcheon, drawing from the field of literary theory, gives us another way of speaking about the "clearing in which psyche and world interpenetrate in a hitherto unknown way." She coins the concept of historiographic metafiction in order to discuss a form of literature that is a "productive problematizing of the entire notion of the relation of language to reality—fictive or historical. Historiographic metafiction both underlines its existence as discourse and yet still posits a relation of reference (however problematic) to the historical world ... Historiographic metafiction always asserts that its world is both resolutely fictive and yet undeniably historical ..." Historiographic metafiction, as a literary form, challenges "the common-sense distinction between two kinds of reference: what history refers to is the actual, real world; what fiction refers to is a fictive universe." Hutcheon, L.: A Poetics of Postmodernism: History, Theory, Fiction. Taylor & Francis, Kindle Edition, 2003, 141-2.

ACKNOWLEDGEMENTS

Epigraphs

Cut Off   Barfield, Owen: (1966). "The Form of Hamlet" in
                    Romanticism Comes of Age. The Barfield Press. San
                    Rafael. (151-2)

Storm   Wrathall, Mark: (2011). *Heiddeger and Unconcealment*.
                    Cambridge University Press. New York (210)

Lisel's Dream   Giegerich, Wolfgang: (2013). *C. G. Jung on Christianity
                    and on Hegel*. Spring Journal Books. New Orleans. (15)

Peter's Nightmare   Guignon, Charles (Ed): (2006). *The Cambridge
                    Companion to Heidegger (Cambridge Companions to
                    Philosophy)*. Cambridge University Press. (369)

Interlocutor   Foucault, Michele: (1971). *The Order of Things*.
                    Pantheon. New York. (306)

Sacrifice   Guignon, Charles (Ed): (2006). *The Cambridge
                    Companion to Heidegger (Cambridge Companions to
                    Philosophy)*. Cambridge University Press. (361-2)

Chaos   Heidegger, Martin: (1976). *Interview with der Spiegel.*

Peter's Demise   Steiner, Rudolph: (1918). *The Work of the Angels in
                    Man's Astral Body*. Zurich. Lecture.
                    "all in all …" is a quote from Pink Floyd.

Decision   Wrathall, Mark: (2011). *Heiddeger and Unconcealment*.
                    Cambridge University Press. New York (210)

Afterword   Ziarek, Krzysztof: (2013). *Language after Heidegger*.
                    Bloomington. Indiana University Press. (14)

ABOUT THE AUTHOR

John C. Woodcock holds a doctorate in
Consciousness Studies (1999). His thesis concerns the
theme of "the end of the world", based on his own
personal experiences lasting twenty years. At first it
seemed to John that he was undergoing a purely
personal psychological crisis but over time he
discovered that he was also participating in the
historical process of a transformation of the soul, as
reflected in the enormous, even apocalyptic, changes
occurring in our culture. During this difficult period of
John's life, he wrote two books: *Living in Uncertainty
Living with Spirit* and *Making of a Man*.

John's next three books, *Transformation of the World*,
The Imperative, and *Hearing Voices*, explore the meaning
of "the end of the world" more fully. John's following
books, including *Animal Soul* and *Manifesting Possible
Futures*, establish a firm theoretical ground for the claim
that the soul is urging us towards the development of
new inner capacities that can help us face the
uncertainty of modern life and, as well, address the
unknown future. His book, *Overcoming Solidity*, continues
this exploration in terms of our current structure of
consciousness and its correlative world of empirical
reality. His book, *Making New Worlds*, begins the work
of articulating the art form that is emerging in response
the soul's intention to incarnate in the real world. He
develops this theme more fully in his book, *The Coming
Guest and the New Art Form*. He has also written an
unusual book, UR-image, which tells a story of four

friends whose lives are interrupted by an intrusion of four possible futures.

John currently lives with his wife Anita in Sydney, where he teaches, writes, and consults with others concerning their own journey through the present "apocalypse of the interior", as it has been called, in his capacity as a practicing Jungian psychotherapist. John and Anita also work with couples in a therapeutic setting.

He may be reached at:

jwoodcock@lighthousedownunder.com